As They Grow

Your One-Year-Old

As They Grow

Your One-Year-Old

By the Editors of Parents Magazine
and Teri Crawford Jones

St. Martin's Griffin ♒ New York

Also by Parents Magazine:
The Parents Answer Book
Parents Magazine's It Worked for Me!
The Parents Party Book
Play and Learn
As They Grow: Your Two-Year-Old
I Can Do It!: Physical Milestones for the First Twelve Months
I Can Do It!: Physical Milestones for One-Year-Olds
I Can Do It!: Physical Milestones for Two-Year-Olds
I Can Do It!: Physical Milestones for Three and Four-Year-Olds

A Roundtable Press Book

For Roundtable Press, Inc.:
Directors: Julie Merberg, Marsha Melnick, and Susan E. Meyer
Project editor: Meredith Wolf Schizer
Consultant: Marge Kennedy
Designer: Laura Smyth
Illustrator: Penny Carter

For Parents Magazine:
Editor-in-chief: Sally Lee
Senior editor: Diane Debrovner
G+J Director of Books and Licensing: Tammy Palazzo

ISBN 0-312-25370-2

First Edition: February 2000

10 9 8 7 6 5 4 3 2 1

Table of Contents

The importance of being me

Your toddler's personality

60

I am some body

Your toddler's sense of self

84

What frightens me   151
Your toddler's fears

Why I do what I do   167
Your toddler's behavior

Foreword

by Sally Lee

How quickly a year goes by! Just yesterday, it seems, you were bringing a precious little bundle home from the hospital, and now that little one is running through the house faster than you can catch up with him (or toddlerproof your home!). One is an age of change. For the first time, you can truly communicate with your baby—he can follow your requests, and thanks to his rapidly expanding vocabulary, you know what's on his mind. While last year's squeals of delight let you know how much he loves you, this year he is capable of even more rewarding signs of affection— true hugs and kisses! At one, your child will also discover friends and develop relationships with other toddlers, a thrilling step towards independence for both of you. His newfound skills, however can overwhelm him, and he may respond with clinging or crying. But be patient—it's all part of being one.

Inside, you'll find a guide to the ups and down of raising a one-year-old. It's bound to be an exhilarating, frustrating, exhausting year, but our expert information will help you— and your toddler—survive and grow during this endlessly fascinating period of his life!

I can do it myself!

Your toddler's emerging sense of independence and mobility

Becoming the parent of a one-year-old is nearly as gratifying and terrifying as *being* a one-year-old. As your child celebrates her first birthday, it's impossible to resist recalling the wondrous details of her emergence from a completely dependent infant to a remarkably competent toddler. You can't help but think back to the moment when she first looked you right in the eye; the day she rolled over unaided; the first time she pulled herself into a sitting position. Surely, you celebrated each new accomplishment, telling her in words and hugs how proud you were to witness each event.

Now, at age one, she's tossing objects across the room with glee; crawling or walking across the room determinedly; tearing off her clothes as soon as you dress her; examining her food carefully right before mashing it into her hair. Like you, your one-year-old is absolutely amazed by her abilities. "Look at what I can do!" she seems to say with every gesture.

Now that her actions can get her into trouble, you may suddenly want to put the brakes on her drive for independence—which until now you have been encouraging wholeheartedly. But when you try to rein her in—for safety's sake, or because you need a respite from running after her—she's likely to react by crying and pulling in the opposite direction.

Your response to your child's push for independence this year will affect her relationship with you and with the world around her in many ways. If you curtail her impulses too frequently, it can reduce her curiosity and damage her self-esteem. If you prohibit her from examining objects and exploring her environment, your child will learn to lean on you for entertainment and direction rather than being able to satisfy herself. She will also learn to mistrust her own ideas and instincts. If she's rarely permitted to exert her will, she may become either compliant and fearful, or rebellious.

On the other hand, if you give your child too much freedom, your toddler may become less adventurous, sensing that no one is looking out for her safety. Of course, allowing her to roam at will can be dangerous as well. Having too much freedom can lead your child to become defiant, because she's looking for boundaries to confirm that she's not *really* the one in charge. Or, if you prod your child into independence before she's ready for it, she'll not only resist your urgings, she will become less likely to venture out when the time is right.

Finding the balance between encouraging your one-year-old's quest for independence and helping her live within the limits you must set is your primary challenge this year.

DEVELOPMENTAL MILESTONE
Mobility

The hallmark of your toddler's growth this year is her newfound mobility, which more than anything else will enable her to establish her independence. Throughout infancy, your child could occupy herself happily just by being in the presence of those she loved. From her crib or bouncy chair, she could explore her hands and feet, grasp a soft toy, watch as you made dinner, and enjoy the antics of pets and siblings. If she looked at an object and made certain noises, you would give her what she wanted or carry her closer for a better look. Your lap was the best place on earth because it gave her a terrific vantage point for exploring while still enveloping her in the safety of your presence.

Beginning at about nine months of age, however, your child's legs and arms grew stronger and her coordination and balance improved. She discovered that, as comfortable as being close to you might be, there were more interesting things to see, better places to go. The urge to explore became overwhelming.

Did you know?
The toddler stage is the only period of development defined by mobility rather than chronological age. The word *toddle* refers to the way in which a child places her feet wide apart to maintain her balance as she walks. A few babies begin to toddle as early as 9 months. Others aren't motivated to walk until 16 months or so. Instead of walking in a heel-to-toe motion like an adult, a toddler places the whole sole of her foot flat on the ground with each step. Her legs are also usually bowed, which makes her gait more wobbly and stiff. For added balance, toddlers extend their arms as they walk.

Tentative rocking on the floor led to crawling. With practice, that crawl became a surefire means of getting from here to there. Holding on to your extended hand or nearby furniture allowed her to experiment with standing upright. Some toddlers skip crawling completely; once they have seen the world from a standing position, nothing less will do. Soon she took her first steps. Now that she could get around on her own, the *desire* to explore and the *ability* to do so merged.

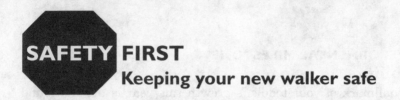

While using a playpen, high chair, or other enclosure is valid for brief periods, such as when you need to accomplish something, it is harmful to limit your toddler's explorations so severely on a regular basis. Your goal is to enlarge the safe areas of your home with careful child-proofing. Within a childproofed environment, your child will *be* safe and *feel* safe. Taking these precautions also allows you to develop a more cooperative rather than combative relationship with your child. To ensure that your home and any other areas that your child spends time in are prepared for her explorations:

• **Hunt for dangerous items.** Walk (and crawl) around your home and try to see everything from your toddler's point of view. What bright colors, small parts, dangling cords, and exposed sockets might attract her attention? If your child can see any hazards, chances are, she can find a way to reach them if she wishes. Remove or cover those things that pose a danger. Tie extra cord lengths together. Place houseplants out of reach. Put locks on cabinets and drawers that contain dangerous items such as medicine, cleansers, or extension cords. Remove scatter rugs and low-to-the-ground decorative items, such as low tables or small statuettes, that your toddler can't easily see from a standing position. Your tour should include items that belong to older siblings as well. Make sure your older child has places to keep his belongings out of his younger sibling's reach.

• **Avoid walkers.** Walkers allow too much freedom of mobility, letting your child fall down steps without the benefit of being able to see them. Studies show that instead of helping toddlers learn to walk, they can actually inhibit the ability because they encourage leg but not hip strength and eliminate the need to learn balance.

• **Reposition furniture.** Remove obstacles such as coffee tables that can interfere with walking. Cover sharp corners. Keep furniture that your toddler can climb on away from windows, shelves, and curtains. Push kitchen and dining-room chairs under the table to prevent your child from using them to reach a tabletop or counter. Lock reclining chairs—which can entrap small climbers—in the upright position or disable them by putting them close to a wall so that the footrests cannot be extended.

• **Secure doors, windows, and stairs.** If you have a swinging door, prop it open with a locking doorstop. A toddler can push open the door, but will not know that the door will then swing back and knock her down, or that it can pinch her fingers. Place safety guards on windows, and child gates at the top and bottom of stairways. Also use gates or securely closed doors to keep your toddler out of the kitchen, bathroom, and any other room where she cannot, even for a moment, explore without you. Place decals on glass doors and windows so that your toddler is aware of their presence.

• **Install safety locks on appliances.** Refrigerators, freezers, washing machines, dryers, and other large appliances make tempting hiding places for toddlers. Make sure that they are unable to open any large appliance. Unplug small appliances such as food processors or can openers when not in use, and install safety latches over easy-to-reach items such as a VCR.

• **Keep your toddler away from water when you are not present.** Water can be fascinating to a toddler who has just learned to walk, run, climb—and splash. If you have a pool, make sure you have adequate fencing around it. Have a guard or lock around the bathtub, toilet, or cleaning bucket. Never leave standing water where your child can get to it. Shut or lock the bathroom door when your child is up and about.

• **Have your child wear the right footwear.** Indoors, let your child go barefoot or wear nonslip socks (if your home is entirely carpeted, your child can wear regular socks instead). Outdoors, dress her in soft, smooth-soled shoes that fit correctly. Smooth soles are less likely to grip and, therefore, trip your child. Don't move on to nonskid soles until she is surer on her feet, at about age two.

The styles and stages of walking

In addition to the flat-footed, wide-legged stance typical of new walkers, many one-year-olds try out a variety of peculiar walking styles. Some try "toe walking," in which they walk on the balls of the feet rather than putting the feet flat on the floor, but usually give up by about 30 months. Some turn their toes inward, while others turn outward, choosing whichever position suits them best. Others experiment with walking only when firmly holding on to you or a piece of furniture; they'll revert to crawling when faced with open spaces.

Early walkers—even those who zip across an open space with ease—are still very much in the learning stage. While their legs may be strong enough to carry them, and their sense of balance improves daily, limitations in their vision and depth perception can lead to accidents. You may find that once your child gets going, she has difficulty stopping or changing direction. Typically, one-year-olds are farsighted. This makes it difficult for them to judge distances. Toddlers also lack spatial awareness, which tells them where their body is in relation to the rest of the world. As a result, your toddler may stumble over obstacles on the floor because she's looking straight ahead and is unaware of anything outside that field of vision. In fact, looking down to see what might be in her way could cause her to lose her balance because tilting her head changes her center of gravity.

Your child's walking and climbing skills will develop in fits and starts. After walking stiff-legged for a month or more, she'll develop a style that includes bending her knees as she toddles. By 18 months, she'll probably be able to lean over and pick up a toy from the floor without sitting down first. Around this time, she will also develop the heel-to-toe motion of walking. Oddly, as her skills increase, your child may actually become less interested in walking and even revert to crawling temporarily if another aspect of development—such as talking or playing with objects that require manual dexterity—interests her more.

Your child's lack of experience can lead her headlong into danger because she'll climb any accessible surface—and seemingly inaccessible ones, too. She'll have more skill at climbing up than getting down and may find herself stuck in precarious situations if you're not there to come to the rescue. Early on, she'll approach sidewalk curbs and stairs with little trepidation, although a fall—in addition to injuring her—could cause her to become more cautious.

By 20 to 24 months, your child may also learn to walk backward a few steps. She may progress from fast walking to running as she develops a smoother, more graceful manner of movement. By the time your toddler approaches her second birthday, she may be able to climb stairs, although she will likely ascend one step at a time, always leading with the same foot, rather than alternating feet. Throughout this year, she may prefer to descend stairs backwards, which allows her to lean over and grasp the stairs themselves for balance.

Mobility and independence
Making decisions about where to go at a given moment is a heady experience for a person who can't yet talk! Being free from your arms, a stroller, or a crib allows your one-year-old to experience a frenzy of freedom. She can reach for the vase and make the water and flowers spill out. She can also find coins to eat, electrical sockets to probe, and can climb to places higher than she can safely descend by herself.

Learning that she can get around on her own naturally encourages your child to experiment with other things that she can do without your help or approval. When you dress her, she can demonstrate how quickly and easily she can undress herself. Or she may decide to run off when she sees that you're about to put on her clothes. When you offer her peas for dinner, she's happy to show you how well she can feed herself—as well as how far she can toss them. Or she may refuse to eat what you serve—even if she's hungry and generally likes the menu—simply for the thrill of asserting herself.

Of course, her emerging assertiveness and self-assurance will also express itself in new abilities to entertain herself and take care of some of her own needs. She might spend a few minutes at a time playing contentedly on her own. She'll show off skills in an effort to please you. For instance, she may hand you her coat as you're getting ready to take her outside, turn the pages of the book you're reading to her, and handle her own spoon during dinner.

Mobility and emotional and cognitive development

The physical ability to move around and explore her surroundings does more than help build your child's muscles. It also profoundly affects her emotional and cognitive development.

When she finds that she can think about an object and retrieve the item she wants all by herself, your child is filled with pride at her abilities. She begins to view herself as a person who can accomplish great things. Encouraged by her success, she then aims to reach higher and walk further. Her ability to walk away from you underscores her own separateness from you. For the first time, she will understand that you, too, are separate from her, but this realization can also produce anxiety.

Her ability to get around on her own also enhances her intellectual development. As she learns to navigate through her environment, she makes many discoveries along the way. Each item she views, reaches for, and grasps adds to her knowledge about the world. She feels textures, such as the cold flat refrigerator door or the rough bark on a tree, that she had not encountered in your arms. She learns from experience, more than from your words, that certain things—the edge of the table or a hot stove—are dangerous and should be avoided. Because she can reach things that once were out of range, she learns more about their properties. She finds out, for example, that paper can be torn or that phones make a sound when you pick them up. The possibilities for discovery are endless.

How it feels to be me

I see something. I want it. And, wonder of wonders, I can get to it all by myself! I don't have to point, or cry, or just hope that you'll pick me up, carry me closer, and show it to me. I have no words yet, so how can I tell you how wonderful it is to be able to go places all by myself? I'll just keep moving. I want to do everything and be everywhere all at once. But, I'm finding out that what I want to do and what I can do don't always go together. And that makes me mad, especially when you say "No" and I really, really, really don't want to stop what I'm doing.

Everything seems new to me. Even something I have seen and held before is new because now I grab it by myself, without your help. Before, you may have helped me to touch it, but now that I can reach it on my own, I can realize how heavy it is and what I can do with it. The neighbor's little dog that I like so much looks different to me when I stand next to it. And, if it barks or jumps, I can get scared because I'm not watching it from your lap like I used to. I don't remember that last time I got in trouble because I touched something I shouldn't touch. All I know is that the world is very tempting. If I like something, I'll go back to it again and again. Each time you say "No!" I remember that I'm not supposed to touch it, but until you say the word, I feel free to explore.

Sometimes there's just too much that's new, and I can't take it all in. Then I get scared, and I need you to hold me. If I know you are always there to help me make sense of the world, then I'll be able to keep trying.

What independence means to your child

Your toddler's push toward independence is a natural one. But just because it's natural doesn't always make it easy for her. As soon as she begins to pull away from you, she learns that there's a price to her newfound independence. Her inward struggle becomes apparent in her struggles with you.

When she notices that she has been playing by herself for a moment while your attention is elsewhere, for instance, she may dissolve into tears out of fear or loneliness. She wants the full attention she has been used to and feels adrift when she realizes that she's depending on herself rather than you for companionship.

With her realization that she can move away from you comes the knowledge that you, too, can move away from her, which can make her excessively clingy and afraid to let you out of her sight. As she experiments with running faster and farther away from you, she needs to know that you will catch up. Running from you is more than an exciting game of chase. When you gather her up, even when you're angry, and you put her into her stroller or high chair despite her protests, your child is reassured that you'll always be there to take care of her.

When you correct her, saying, "Don't touch!" or "No!" it's probably her first experience with your displeasure. (While it's true that you may have stopped her from hair-pulling or biting while nursing with a firm "No" earlier on, she has no memory of these events.) Being mobile gives her many more opportunities to wander into prohibited territory. Your reprimands often confuse and frighten her.

At the same time, your child is learning the power she has to affect you. When she pulls at an electrical cord and you jump up and shout "Don't!" she sees for the first time how easily she can control you. If she bursts into tears when you correct her, she may feel a mixture of sadness for having displeased you and apprehension. After all, if she can control you, are you still able to protect her? She wants to know that the one in charge is you, not her.

Your child may not always like the results of her newfound mobility and the independence it allows. For the first time in her life, you may insist that your child walk from one place to another when she would prefer to be carried. If you refuse to pick her up, she may go limp and simply plop herself down wherever she is. She has decided right then and there that the ability to walk comes with too high a price. If you pick her up, she may confuse you by struggling just a moment later to be allowed down again. She's not being defiant or intentionally contrary. She simply lives in the moment, and what she wants one moment can be very different from what she wants the next.

YOU AND YOUR CHILD
Adjusting to your toddler's independence
Your child isn't the only one who experiences a conflict between her need for independence and her dependency on you. No doubt, there are days when you'll wish you could turn back the clock and reclaim your child's infancy. Or, now that your child is mobile, you may be eager to put the baby days behind you quickly. But neither holding your toddler back nor rushing her along is possible. During this year, you'll find that the best pace for growing and gaining independence is the one your child sets. And every two steps forward may involve two steps back as well.

How easy or difficult you perceive this year to be depends largely on how prepared you are for the changes in your role as a parent now that your baby is a toddler. If you see your child's mobility and emerging independence as an invitation to explore the world with her, then you will find this stage particularly rewarding. As you see the world through your child's eyes, you can join in her excitement at each new discovery. Empathizing with her also helps you understand her frustrations. Even though she seems to understand everything you say, she can't always remember your directives from one moment to the next. If you realize this, you'll be less likely to think her misbehavior is deliberate. You won't resent the expense of energy that you must spend on her now when you recognize that the combination of her mobility and limited judgment requires your constant vigilance. Her ability to explore new areas brings her into contact with things she has not yet experienced, so she has no frame of reference for what may be dangerous to her.

Difficulties in your relationship with your toddler generally stem from a mismatch between your expectations and your child's capabilities. Also, differences between you and your child's inherent personalities can hinder an easy relationship. (For more on temperament, see Chapter 3.) The exhaustion that comes from running after a toddler naturally takes its toll, too. How can you ensure that your relationship with your toddler develops into a cooperative rather than a combative one? By giving her as much freedom as possible within boundaries that serve you both.

HELPING YOUR CHILD GROW
Nurturing independence

Your one-year-old strives to be independent—but she still wants your help. In other words, it's up to you to interpret when to step back and when to offer assistance. It's nearly impossible to read her signals correctly 100 percent of the time, but careful observation of your child will allow you to be more in tune with her temperament and moods and to better anticipate her needs. There are many things you can do to be there for your child as you encourage her explorations.

Give her wide spaces in which to walk, run, and climb. Childproofed indoor areas allow her to explore freely and reduce your need to say "No!" each time she reaches for an object that's off-limits. Outdoors, look for open spaces, away from traffic and big-kid playground equipment. The object is to enable your child to put some distance between herself and you without causing either of you too much anxiety. If you always remain right by her side, hovering over her every move, you are telling your child that you don't entirely trust her abilities, which, in turn, undermines her self-confidence.

Remain in view. Don't take her walking (and running!) away from you as a cue that she doesn't need your presence, however. Your child needs to know that, although she can run away, you remain available. One of her favorite activities, of course, will be to have you chase her around your house and yard. If you cannot restrict her run times to places that are securely enclosed, your best approach is to remind her firmly that she must stay within the limits you have determined. Upon retrieving her, say, "I need to be able to see you to keep you safe. If you run away again, I'll have to put you in your stroller." Then, if she takes off again, remind her of your warning and follow through by restricting her movements for a time.

Most of the time you'll find that your child isn't really interested in moving far away from you—she simply wants to see how far you'll let her go. By observing her explorations, you may notice that she is entirely aware of where you are and how well you are keeping track of her, even as she takes off. You'll see that she constantly checks on you with a quick glance and is reassured when she sees that you are still looking. You may even discover that she has set for herself a perimeter beyond which she won't go. By testing her environment and taking her cues from you as to what is safe or not safe, she begins to internalize the boundaries you have set for her.

Give practice with separation. Even if you wanted to, it's unlikely that you can spend all of your child's waking time in her presence. Your child therefore needs some practice separating from you and then enjoying reunions with you. In addition to the brief separations your child orchestrates when she runs from you or when she becomes engaged in an activity without you, she needs to feel secure in another's presence. Your child may have already experienced some form of day care and may be used to it. But if not, now is the time; you also need the opportunity to take a break. Even though occasionally there will be some tears, take regular breaks from each other, leaving your child in other capable and loving hands. Experiences in separation will teach your child that she can cope and can even thrive in a variety of circumstances. Being cared for by others assures your child that the world beyond your arms is a safe and welcoming place.

Provide opportunities for exploration and discovery. Your toddler's sense of adventure does not always require a large area. While restricting access to any cabinets and drawers that contain potentially dangerous items, be sure that not every interesting corner of each room is off-limits. In the kitchen, rearrange some storage spaces so that a low cabinet contains plastic bowls, pots and pans, spoons, and measuring cups she can play with. In the bedrooms, you might store socks in an open basket that your child can dump out and refill. (Don't make a non-built-in dresser drawer accessible unless you are there to supervise. To keep a toddler from pulling open drawers, possibly toppling the dresser, use drawer locks or latches, or bolt the dresser to the wall.) Elsewhere in the house, place some of your child's books and toys within her easy reach. The ability to get to items of interest, even those that are behind closed doors or somewhat out of reach, gives your child experiences in satisfying her own curiosity. This, in turn, enhances her sense of self-reliance, a positive aspect of independence, and one you'll want to encourage.

Guide, but don't take over when playing. There's certainly nothing wrong with showing your child how a toy or other object is designed to be used. But when she has other ideas—wanting to use her toy telephone as a truck, for instance—it's important to let your child pursue her play in her own way. When you introduce your child to a plaything that does require clear rules for use, such as crayons, state the rules clearly and stay within range so that you can be sure they aren't misused.

Praise, but don't go overboard. Although it may not always be apparent to you, your toddler wants nothing more than to please you. Be careful to avoid criticizing your child, who may be more sensitive than you would think. A word of encouragement and a show of admiration for a task well done or a sincere attempt boosts her confidence. She feels enormously proud when she earns your congratulations. As important as your praise is to her, it's vital that you don't overdo it, especially for skills that your child is not working particularly hard at. For instance, if she's an able and practiced stair walker and you tell her each time she manages a step just how terrific she is, she might become afraid of trying anything new for fear that by making a mistake she might lose your favor. In order to learn, she needs the freedom to fail and to try again. Focus your praise on the effort and on the specific task by saying such things as "You're working hard to climb those steps." and "You climbed three steps all by yourself. You must be very proud." What is most important is that the praise be sincere.

Share in the fun. Your toddler has a ball as she explores every nook and cranny of her home. When you get down on the floor with her to help examine all her discoveries, you add tremendously to her enjoyment. While walking up and down two steps repeatedly may not be on the top of your list, to your toddler, such a repetitive activity is great fun and allows her to practice and enhance her skills. So, whenever she appears to want you to join in her games, do so. Otherwise, be ready to watch and cheer her on.

Allow some frustration. If your toddler appears to be struggling with how to stack blocks, try to let her test out different ways of solving the problem rather than stepping in and showing her how it's done. There may be times, however, when she may not recognize her need for your assistance and, in those cases, it's up to you to determine when to intervene. For example, your one-year-old may be determined to move a chair to get to a toy that is under it, but may find herself unable to do so. You can wait a moment to see if she is pausing to figure out her next move or if she's about to break out in tears of frustration or fear. Approach the situation by asking rather than just swooping in. If you say, "It looks like you're trying to get that toy. Do you need some help moving the chair?" your child will let you know what she needs from you.

Don't hesitate to set limits. For your child to establish the independence she'll enjoy for a lifetime, she needs the security that boundaries provide now. The more comfortable you are with setting limits on how far she can go—both in distance and in behavior—the more comfortable she will be exploring within the reasonable limits you set. (For more on setting limits, see Chapter 8.)

Expect some regression. As your toddler gains more experience with independent movement, and more control over her actions, sudden bursts of clinginess may come as a surprise to you. Is the child who's wrapped securely around your leg or pleading to be picked up the same child who, just a moment ago, was running off with you in hot pursuit? Yes, of course, and both the running and the retreat are part of her development. As she begins to understand just how independent she's becoming, her return to you allows her to reassure herself that she's not too independent yet. Moreover, she needs to be reminded that no matter how self-sufficient she's becoming, you're still there for her when she needs to check in. Your patience will give her the reassurance she needs and the courage to venture out again.

Schedule enough time for necessary tasks. Things you once were able to accomplish in a relatively brief time—like getting your child dressed in the morning—will take longer now that your child is a toddler because she'll want to do things herself. The pay-off for allowing her enough time to learn these skills will come in a few years when your child can competently handle some self-care routines on her own, without your input.

Errands with a toddler in tow can take far longer as your child wants to walk a bit and examine everything along the way. When planning any activity, schedule more time than you did in the past or, if time is tight, try to arrange for someone else to watch your child while you run your errands.

Include quiet time. As important as providing the active, physical play your toddler needs, don't forget to include quiet activities, too. Cuddling quietly or snuggling up with a book gives both you and your child the opportunity to regroup, to settle down, and to take in all that was learned by more active pursuits.

The importance of routines

By establishing daily routines, you provide your child with a secure sense that her world is dependable and predictable. Routines around major daily events, eating, getting ready to go out, bathing, and sleeping, eliminate the need for you to create rules throughout the day. They also reduce your child's need to test limits as she strives to establish her independence. If she knows, for instance, that her bedtime routine always includes a bath, a story, and a song, then she is far less likely to continue exploring once the routine has begun. Routines must be long enough—at least ten minutes—to establish a pattern of behavior, and short enough—no more than half an hour—to discourage deviation from them. Sometimes routines can be quick, like a silly song that you sing before leaving the house. To make it a routine, be sure to do it every time.

Within your daily routine, you should have some flexibility, however. For example, if your child's bath usually takes fifteen minutes, but she discovers a new way to splash on a particular night, let her enjoy practicing her new skill for a few extra minutes if she wants to, rather than adhering to your timetable. (For more on routines, see pp. 76, 163–64, and 172.)

If your child...	Do say	Don't say
wants to button her own sweater	"You're learning how to button! Good for you!"	"That's too hard for you. Let me do it."
struggles to put a shape block into a shape sorter	"Try another hole and see if that works."	"It goes in like this."
wants to handle an off-limits object	"That's for looking at, not for touching. Would you like me to help you get a closer look?"	"No! Never touch that!"
runs off from you in a playground	"I need to be able to see you to keep you safe. If you run away again, I'll have to put you in your stroller."	"Bad girl! Don't run from me."
tosses her food	"Food is for eating." (If she continues tossing it, remove it until she's hungrier and more inclined to eat it.)	"Don't do that."

Great physical activities for toddlers
In addition to the running, jumping, and climbing activities your toddler discovers for herself, try these games and activities:

♦ Blow soap bubbles for your child to chase.

♦ Place a board on the ground and encourage her to walk across to help her learn balance.

♦ Give your child opportunities to imitate your movements while following simple commands. For example, tell her to "point to the sky, now touch the ground, turn in a circle, and now sit down."

♦ Walk barefoot with your toddler on a variety of surfaces—the grass, sand, carpet, pillows, wood—and talk about how they feel.

♦ Put on some lively music and dance with your toddler.

♦ Let your child roll around with her tummy placed on a large sturdy ball, with you holding her and guiding the movements.

♦ Place pillows on the floor for your child to bounce and fall on. Arrange others so that she will have a soft landing if she topples.

♦ Make a tunnel out of a large box. Cut off the flaps on both ends, making sure there are no staples left in the cardboard. The box will be fun for your child to crawl through.

♦ Play games such as ring-around-a-rosy and hide-and-seek. Hide both yourself (where your child can easily find you) and objects.

♦ Slightly wild lap and arm rides such as "This is the way the lady rides…," will thrill your toddler as they give her a more dramatic sense of movement than she could create on her own.

What I'm trying to say is...

Your toddler's language development

Just as learning to walk allows your child to experience a new level of independence, developing language lets him reach a new level of socializing. The growth of a toddler's language skills begins with the expansion of his listening vocabulary. He can follow directions, handing you something you request, for example, or stop in his tracks, at least for a second or two, when you say, "No." Clearly, his brain power is stimulated by language as he learns to link your spoken words with objects, actions, and feelings that are familiar to him.

At around one year, your child's babbles evolve into a few understandable syllables. Though his initial vocalizing is nothing more than practicing random sounds, he decides to try to imitate sounds he has heard, and he learns quickly that certain syllables garner a positive reaction. When he babbles "mamama," you respond with a congratulatory "You said Mama!" Delighted at the attention the sound earns him, he says it again and again. It's no longer a random sound. Now, it's intentional and meant to communicate. This opens the door to two-way conversation, the give and take that he will experiment with this year and his whole life.

Learning to communicate with words boosts your child's self-confidence in addition to granting him a new, important place among other people. With words, he can express his likes and dislikes, his joys and upsets.

DEVELOPMENTAL MILESTONE
Spoken language

Few one-year-olds master the art of conversation, but this year your child is gearing up for just that. As with any stage of development, children acquire spoken language at different rates, some forming recognizable and understandable words by the age of 10 months or so, and others not until their third birthday. However, most children go through predictable stages and achieve certain milestones during the first two years.

To see where your child is heading now, it's important to look back at the earliest stages of language development. During his first few months, as your infant listened to you and others talk—especially when it was directed at him—he associated voices with comfort. By just a few weeks of age, he was able to distinguish different voices, preferring higher pitched tones to lower ones. He listened to you in the womb and recognized your voice his first day. By three months or earlier, he turned toward your voice and was soothed by your talking or singing to him. He babbled and made gurgling sounds, particularly in response to your talking to him.

Between three and six months, he learned to distinguish happy tones of voice from harsh ones and became upset by an angry voice. At this point, his babbling began to take on the cadence—the rhythms and inflections—of his native language. He also knew how to get your attention by vocalizing and was delighted when you responded to his sounds with words of your own. He may have carried on "conversations" with you as long as you talked to him face to face. When alone, he may have talked to himself—making sounds, then stopping, then answering himself in the same give-and-take pattern you used when you talked to him. By eight months, he was probably able to focus on conversations, even when he was not a part of them. At this point, he may have found a way to interrupt these conversations with a companionable shout to get your attention.

A big change came at about nine months. In addition to responding simply to the sound of your voice, your child paid particular attention when you called his name or when you named objects or people that were familiar to him—proof that he had learned to associate particular sounds with specific meanings. At this point, your child may have started to string together a variety of babbling syllables that he repeated over and over, combining them in different ways. This process is commonly called "jargoning," which—because it repeats a set of syllables and rhythm—sounds like a distinct language. By 10 to 12 months, your baby may have a learned a few words—usually Dada and Mama—that are recognizable to others. "No" is also an easy word to say and becomes a favorite for a variety of reasons: It allows him to express his opinions, it gets a reaction from you, and he probably has had lots of experience hearing it. By the end of his first year, his listening vocabulary most likely has grown to contain 20 or more words.

Your one-year-old still relies heavily on sounds, gestures, and facial expressions to communicate. However, at this age, his listening vocabulary is growing rapidly. If he has started to say real words, he may combine these words with jargoning that mimics the pattern of sentences.

Your child's first words will reflect his experiences and the things and people who are most important to him. Generally, first words fall into basic categories. These categories include *names,* in addition to Mama and Dada, such as a sibling or pet's name and important *objects* such as "ball" and "cookie"; *action words* such as "eat" and "go"; *requests* such as "more" or "up"; and personal or *social words,* such as "bye-bye," "hi," and "No."

The words your child chooses give you a window into how his mind is working. For example, he is learning to categorize when he uses the word *dog* to name all animals, but would never use the word *dog* to describe a vehicle. To refer to vehicles, he might choose the word *car.* Just as your child may overgeneralize, he might also restrict the meanings of some words. For example, he may correctly use the word *book* (perhaps pronouncing it "booh") to refer to one special book he enjoys hearing, but he doesn't use this word to describe any other book.

At first, your child may say only part of a word, cutting off the first or last syllable, or leaving off a consonant at the end of a word, such as "ba" for "ball" and "oo" or "tu" for "shoe." He may have a problem using two different consonants in one word, so that instead of saying *dog,* he may say, "daw" or "dawd." Certain consonants and combinations of letters are especially difficult for children to learn. Many kids don't master all the consonant sounds, especially *s, z, th, r,* and *f,* until kindergarten age.

At about 15 months, you may notice your child's vocabulary development slowing down. It's common for toddlers to postpone further speech development while they're busy mastering other physical skills. Your toddler will likely continue practicing words and word sounds, using jargon in conversation, but he won't add many words to his vocabulary for a few months. Because his ability to form ideas and mental pictures continues full-speed ahead, however, he'll become frustrated when he is unable to make himself and his thoughts clear to you. He'll increasingly insist that you pay attention to what he's trying to say, and may pull you across the room by the hand to bring you closer to the thing he wants to discuss. If what he wants to say cannot be explained with body language, he may have a tantrum.

Although your toddler is likely to take a breather from attempting to talk at around 15 months, this does not indicate that your child's language development has shut down. He now has a heightened interest in listening, which, when he's ready to verbalize again, will serve him well. He may become transfixed by watching and listening to children's television shows in which the language and visuals are geared toward young children. He may sing the melody of a song that you recognize without the words. When you talk to him, he pays particular attention to your words, listening carefully to identify emphasis. For instance, if you're about to feed him and you hand him his spoon, saying, "Hold your own spoon now," he'll hear your emphasis on the word *spoon* and learn to associate it with the object you're handing him.

Speech development regains your toddler's attention at about 18 months. From now through his second birthday, your child will probably acquire a speaking vocabulary ranging from 50 to 200 words. It's important to note that these "words" may not be identifiable to others. For instance, your toddler may say "ha," which you both know means "hat," but may not be considered a spoken word by another listener. It qualifies as a word, however, because it is a sound that consistently stands for a particular object.

Picture books in which your child can point to pictures that you name are especially meaningful and enjoyable because they give him a way to convey his understanding of many words without having to pronounce them in the standard way. He may not be able to say "horse," but if you say, "Point to the horse," he can readily do so. Opportunities to demonstrate his understanding reinforce his desire to talk. Conversations in which you ask, "Where's your head?" or say, "Bring me your slippers" are thrilling to your toddler because they prove to him that he's now a partner in this communication game.

During this stage, your toddler will begin to put together phrases such as "more cookie" or "me down," using nouns and modifiers in the correct sequence. He may say only the most important words to get the meaning across, leaving out "a" and "the," prepositions such as "in," and many word endings.

In addition to talking about his immediate experiences, your toddler may also begin to talk about things and people who are not present, again giving you insight into the more complex workings of his brain. For example, he may ask about a family member who is not at home, saying something like, "Where cat?" when he enters the living room and doesn't see his cat on its usual perch on the sofa. At around 21 months, your toddler may construct two-word sentences, now using verbs and nouns or pronouns, such as "Me go" or "Mommy eat." He may also begin to ask questions about the names of things and start to enjoy simple word games. Nursery rhymes with repetitive words and phrases delight him because he enjoys hearing familiar words over and over. At this stage, it becomes easier for your child to describe his feelings; he may try to tell you what is wrong before dissolving into tears. He may extend a hurt finger to you, saying "Kiss boo-boo" to let you know what he needs to feel better.

By age two, although actual vocabulary such as verbs and adjectives are still beyond his reach, he'll speak in longer sentences, using his own words or jargon in a variety of parts of speech. He'll become more adept at asking questions, not just to gain specific information, but simply for the pleasure of continuing a conversation with you.

Factors that affect language development
Children are born "hardwired" with the capacity for language. One factor in language development is your child's personality. Some children are naturally more talkative and interested in language than others. They focus on real words and are eager to mimic them. Others enjoy the sounds of language and its social uses, but

are content to use jargon rather than focus on pronunciation. Some children—often boys—are more focused on being physical than verbal. Although all children learn to talk in the same stages—starting with words, progressing to phrases, and then to sentences—they don't do so at the same rate. In fact, an early talker may not be the first child in a group to use sentences. A late talker may progress more quickly through the stages from words to using sentences. Late talkers may also pronounce words more clearly and have a greater vocabulary from the start.

Being an early talker or a late talker is not an indication of your child's intelligence. Some children will take more risks and try out language at an earlier age. Others will be more cautious and won't begin to talk regularly until they are sure they have a good sense of how to do so. Other factors that influence language development include:

Environment. Research has shown that the environment in which a child grows up greatly affects how readily he learns to speak. Lots of exposure to conversation encourages a child to join in the act. If you frequently talk to and interact with your toddler, making eye contact and responding verbally to his babbles, you will enhance his speech development, even if he doesn't say words himself until later on. On the other hand, if you are highly attuned and responsive to your toddler's body language and jargoning, he may see no need to improve his language skills right now. Toddlers who attend quality child-care programs tend to speak earlier because so much language is directed at them by teachers and older children, and the usefulness of being able to express themselves is so clear in social situations that encourage verbal interaction. Delays in both language and intellectual development occur when a child is rarely spoken to or his babbles are largely ignored.

If your child grows up in a bilingual household, there may be some delay in vocabulary development in both languages. Throughout age one, he may mix words and syntax from the two languages, but by the time he's about two, he will have learned to distinguish one from the other, eventually becoming fluent in both.

Attention to other development. If your child was an early walker who went on to become physically active in a number of ways—climbing, jumping, and throwing balls—you may find that he is a late talker. With all this activity, he may have little time or energy left over for exploring words.

Heredity. Genetics play a part in your child's language development. If either parent was an early or late talker, your child may have inherited that tendency.

Family placement. First and only children, who have their parents' full attention, tend to be earlier talkers. But later children also have an advantage if an older sibling regularly engages the younger one in playful conversation. However, an older sibling may also be better able to interpret what a toddler is saying so that the younger child is less motivated to talk for himself.

Gender. Girls tend to talk earlier than boys. However, many researchers believe that this may be because parents engage their daughters in conversation more often than they do their sons. Boys tend to be more physical than girls, which also may be reinforced by parents' behavior.

What if there seems to be a delay?

It is too early to judge if your child has a speech delay. But speech is only one aspect of language development. The other is listening and understanding. If your toddler doesn't appear to be at all interested in the language around him, doesn't respond to spoken language or other sounds, or rarely babbles, he may suffer from a hearing loss. (See box, p. 38.) Malformations of the mouth that had not been diagnosed and corrected in infancy can also lead to a delay in speaking.

Hearing impairment: What to look for

An estimated three percent of school-age children have some form of hearing impairment, from minimal loss to deafness. Moderate to severe impairment is nearly always diagnosed by age one during regular checkups. Minimal loss can be harder to detect.

If your toddler is unresponsive to sounds, responds only to high pitches or loud noises, or if he rarely babbles and doesn't try to engage you verbally, have his hearing checked by a pediatrician, who may refer you to an audiologist. One of the most common reasons for temporary hearing loss is ear infections. Other children at high risk of hearing loss, and who need to be carefully monitored, include those who have been diagnosed with a medical problem (such as Franconi syndrome); have a family history of hearing disorders; were exposed to rubella or another virus in utero; weighed less than three pounds, four ounces at birth; were born with an abnormality of the face or ears; had a low APGAR score at birth; experienced seizures or a serious illness during infancy; or have allergies. Children who have had any head injury are also at high risk of developing a hearing loss.

A sign that your child's hearing could be slightly impaired is if he gives inappropriate answers to questions or cannot follow verbal directions. If he consistently turns one ear toward the source of a sound—showing that he clearly favors that ear—his hearing should be evaluated. Other symptoms of hearing loss include an inability to distinguish between words that sound similar, such as door and store; an inability to detect tones in the voice that express different emotions such as anger and sadness; pulling on the ears or complaining of pain in an ear; and "babbling" with his hands in an organized way without speaking. These movements may appear to be very similar to the jargon and baby signs of a toddler who hears normally.

Speech therapy and treatment—including medication, surgery, hearing aids, and/or special educational intervention—can help all degrees of hearing loss. The earlier hearing impairment is diagnosed and treated, the less likely it is to result in a language or learning delay.

A delay could have nonphysical causes. A major change in your child's environment and routine, such as a move or a new caregiver or sibling, can disrupt your child's development temporarily. Putting pressure on your child to talk before he's ready can also backfire and inhibit him from expressing himself verbally.

Body language

Until your child has a better command of spoken language, he will rely on body language to communicate with those around him. Carefully observing your toddler's physical communication style will allow you to keep your end of the conversation going more smoothly. You will also respond better to your child's behavior.

Facial expressions are the best clues about your child's moods. As you mirrored your child's expressions during his infancy— smiling when he smiled and frowning when he frowned—he discovered that these expressions could communicate moods. He learned to smile to get your positive attention rather than to show that he felt happy. The universality of using and responding to broad smiles and pouting frowns leaves little room for misinterpretation. But nuances in facial expressions can indicate a wider variety of feelings.

Smiles. In addition to happiness, smiles can signal uncertainty, anxiety, or even anger. A wide, open-mouthed smile showing both upper and lower teeth that includes wrinkles under the eyes is a real sign of pleasure or amusement. Raised eyebrows and a smile indicate surprise and excitement. A wide open mouth covering the teeth generally suggests a relaxed and playful mood. A closed-mouth, tight-lipped smile can signal embarrassment if a child is nearing his second birthday or can be used at people or things that are new and interesting but not quite in your child's comfort zone. When only the upper teeth are uncovered, the smile is friendly. When a smile shows only the lower teeth, it signals aggression.

Frowns. When your child's lower lip extends outward, he's sad. When a frown is accompanied by a furrowed brow, it can signal confusion, while a smooth forehead may mean lack of interest. A frown with squinting eyes indicates anger or dismay.

Hand and arm signals. No doubt your child has developed a few gestures that clue you in to his needs. Raised arms are a call to be picked up. Clinging to your leg is a clear sign that he's uncomfortable with a situation and needs to be held and reassured. If your child holds his arms stiffly at his side, he may feel anxious about something. He may also express anxiety by rubbing his hands together, stroking his face, or by chewing on his fingers. A clenched fist may mean your child is fearful, while limp hands generally indicate tiredness. Putting his hands over his eyes can show playfulness during a game of peekaboo, but in other contexts, it can mean apprehension or anxiety, and is simply a way for your child to remove himself from a situation.

Stance. How your child holds his body has meaning, too. Bending forward with his head lowered, along with an angry stare and clenched fists, can signal aggression. If his head and upper body are bent forward and he smiles and looks at someone directly, your child is showing a desire for friendship. If he leans back and has a playful expression, he is having fun. Walking or standing stiffly, especially with lowered eyes, can reveal anxiety, as when your child is first introduced to a new person or group.

Some gestures—nodding his head to mean yes or shaking it from side to side to mean no—are responses your child learned early on and ones you can be pretty sure mean exactly what they say. However, many toddlers delight in saying "No," both verbally and with a head shake, just because it gets a reaction. For instance, if you playfully ask your child, "Are you cute?" he may respond with a fervent head shake, while smiling broadly—indicating that saying "No," however it's done, is great fun.

Other gestures are less clear. For example, if your child hands you something that has sparked his interest, you may interpret this gesture as a form of gift giving and thank him for it. However, the concept of giving a present to please someone else isn't understood until the age of two, or later. When your toddler hands you an object, it is his way of saying, "Look at this interesting thing. Tell me about it."

Gestures can also be misinterpreted as misbehaviors. If, for example, your toddler grabs a toy from a playmate, you may be quick to rush in to correct him, saying, "It's not nice to grab." But your child will be confused because he never intended to make his playmate—or you—unhappy. He just wanted to to see it, to touch it. You might try saying, "I know you want to look at the toy. Your friend has the toy now. Let's ask your friend if you can look at it." You will probably have to repeat variations on these words frequently, as your toddler is unlikely to remember that he must ask first. When he sees something interesting, his only thought is to get a closer look, to touch, and to explore. If his playmate is unwilling to give up or share the toy, which is likely, you may have to try to redirect your child to another interesting object or toy.

Toddlers will also use physical actions, such as biting, to communicate anger and frustration. They are not trying to hurt another person, they simply aren't able to say, "I'm too tired to think clearly." (For tips on dealing with biting and other nonverbal signals, see p. 184.)

Your child's body language will give you insight into the range of his receptive language—his listening vocabulary—since his reactions to your words let you know what he does, and doesn't, understand. For example, you might ask your child, "Where is your nose?" or "Show me your kitty." When your child points to his nose or points to and picks up his stuffed cat toy, you know that he has understood what you said, even though he may not be able to say nose or kitty for several more months.

In communicating with your toddler, pay attention to your own body language, too. Because your toddler depends so greatly on gestures before he has mastered the spoken word, he will "read" your body language first, and then listen to what you're saying. That's why getting down on your child's level, giving a warm, reassuring hug, and having direct eye contact is often much more important than the words you use. Matching your body language to the meaning of your words is essential, not only to your child's speech development but to his emotional health. If you were to speak in a friendly, inviting way, but physically remained aloof, your child would be confused. Likewise, if you used harsh words while acting in a loving way, your child would be torn between depending on words or gestures to make sense of your mood. When your gestures and words are in sync, you enhance your child's ability to adopt the words as his own. Matching words and motions also reinforces your child's trust in your emotions, and thus his own.

Your child will learn to read your gestures before he can learn to read others'. For this reason, he may behave shyly when strangers talk directly to him simply because he doesn't understand their particular body language. A person who doesn't have the same gestures, expressions, and way of talking that you do isn't, in your child's opinion, speaking in a language he understands.

Introducing "Baby Signs"

There's no need to wait until your child has a larger speaking vocabulary to engage in active communication with him. Toddlers, it's been shown, are adept at learning a form of sign language that can aid in conversing long before they have the words to do so. Unlike the body language gestures that come naturally to you and your child, you can teach this form of signing in a conscious way. Developed by Linda Acredolo, Ph.D., a professor of psychology at the University of California, Davis, and Susan Goodwyn, Ph.D., associate professor of psychology at California State University in Stanislaus, this method of communication is called Baby Signs. Baby Signs includes a number of gestures that signal objects, events, or ideas that you and your toddler can make to represent words. You and your toddler can create additional and/or different signals to discuss things and ideas that are meaningful to him. The key is to use the signs whenever you discuss the object or idea so that your toddler learns to associate each gesture with its corresponding word. The examples shown below are those that the researchers have developed.

Baby signs

Caterpillar	A wiggling finger
Hippopotamus	A mouth opened wide
Birds	Arms flapping up and down
Flower	A sniffing motion
Piano	Fingers moving up and down as in playing a piano
Book	Placing the hands next to each other, palms up, and making an opening and closing gesture
I'm sleepy	Two hands pressed together by one ear
I'm cold	Hugging oneself
I want more	Pointing one finger into the palm of the other hand
I'm afraid	Tapping the chest
It is noisy	Pointing to one ear
I want to go out	Turning a hand as though turning a doorknob

When introducing Baby Signs, it's best to start with only a few, and then add others as your child grows more "fluent." Choose simple motions that are easy to perform, understand, and remember. When signing, also say the word to help your child make the connection between the gesture and the word. When your child begins to mimic the signs you have taught him, use words to accompany his signing. For example, if he points a finger into the palm of his hand, say, "You want more." Use the signs you have already introduced frequently to reinforce their meaning and to encourage your child to use the signs to converse with you.

Signing has a variety of benefits. Acredolo and Goodwyn found that children who are taught to sign are able to communicate earlier. They are encouraged to listen, to work at comprehending what they hear, and to find things to "talk" about. Signing has also been found to improve attention span, encourage an interest in reading, boost self-esteem, and give siblings a fun and entertaining way to communicate with a younger child. Signing will also give you tremendous insight into your child's thinking and what interests him long before he has the words to share his ideas with you verbally.

How it feels to be me

When you talk to me and really listen to me talk back to you, I feel special. I like the sounds of our voices. When you understand what I say, even when I'm not using words, I feel like I have done something wonderful. I can tell that you're excited by our conversations, too.

There is so much that I want to share and tell you about. But it's so hard to say what I mean when I don't have the right words. And when I use the words I'm trying to pronounce and you don't understand me, I get upset sometimes. I recognize many of the words you say to me, but I just don't know how to say them back yet. But, please keep talking to me. Listening to you, and having you listen to me, is the best way for me to learn how to talk. And then, I can tell you everything that's on my mind.

CONFLICT
What speaking in words means to your child

Learning to talk creates a see-saw of emotion for your toddler. On the one hand, he enjoys the new power, especially when a word from him garners a reaction from you. He says "Up," and you lift him. He calls the cat by its name and you cheer. And he's sure to get a reaction when he says "No!" His play style is enhanced as he babbles and chats with his toys, imagining all the while a conversation between his stuffed tiger and his truck. Language is a delight, and he's enjoying just about every syllable of it.

On the other hand, when his attempts to talk do not result in your understanding, language can be a source of frustration. When he babbles, uses jargon, or mispronounces as he speaks, your child is certain of what it is he wants to communicate. The problem for him lies with how you and others interpret his speech. When his words don't work as he wants them to, he must resort to more acting out to express himself. His fury gets a response, and this creates something of a dilemma for him: Does he continue practicing words even when he's not getting his message across or does he continue to resort to babyish cries and gestures to be heard? Because his impulse is always to move forward, even with some backsliding, your child will, of course, pursue his interest in speaking.

Once he has acquired a few words, your child may be content to practice those words again and again, feeling no need for a larger vocabulary for a time. He'll be annoyed and possibly resistant to your urgings if you suddenly insist that he use words instead of the gestures that have worked pretty well for him up until now. Just as learning to walk meant that you sometimes insisted that he not be carried, now he has to contend with the fact that you may expect words when he's not in the mood for chatter. As with any new skill, your child learns that moving ahead with language comes with a price.

How language affects your relationship

Of course, you'll be eager to hear your child tell you the many things that are on his mind. When he can say a word or two, you may be ready to put the gesturing behind you and move full throttle toward real conversation. Naturally, you're frustrated if you're unable to interpret most or even any of his verbalizations. You sense your child's frustration, too. For the first time, it seems like you're like two tourists who have just met, each speaking a different language, instead of the intimate pair that you have been until now.

It's an odd thing that the onset of spoken language places a communication barrier between you and your toddler. You both have raised expectations of communicating but the reality of casual banter and thoughtful conversations is still off in the future. You may notice that other toddlers are at a different stage in their acquisition of language and may feel that you need to encourage your child to speed up if he's not talking as much or as well as his peers. It's important to remember that speaking, like all other aspects of development, will proceed at the pace that's right for your child. Becoming overly concerned with his rate of adding new words to his vocabulary or with his pronunciations is not productive. The more you simply enjoy the pace your child has set, the more easily you can join him in his travels into the speaking world. You can provide the map by continuing to speak to him about everything around him, but he should do the steering.

When your toddler does begin to talk, your first reactions are undoubtedly excited ones. You're thrilled at his first naming words—*mama, dada, cat*. When he moves into the next stage, your child is likely to give a real workout to the word *no*. This gets him an entirely different reaction. That, combined with his ability to run away from you, give you and your child your first experiences with disagreements. You may see these confrontations as signs that your easy-to-manage baby is developing into a defiant toddler. In reality, he's just practicing new skills, testing himself while testing you. If you keep your responses firm and loving, he'll more readily move on to other areas of development rather than testing how far he can push you. Your continued patience and understanding will free him to move on to other things.

HELPING YOUR CHILD GROW
Encouraging language development
Language development is really a three-part learning process. First, there's vocabulary development, a mental process that includes acquiring a listening and speaking vocabulary. This process allows your child to make sense of language and to show what he knows about words and ideas. Second, there's speech and pronunciation. This is a physical process that includes listening and processing sounds, and shaping the mouth to mimic those sounds. Third, there are the social aspects of language—what to say, when to speak, how to converse in acceptable ways.

Vocabulary development
The more your child hears language—in conversations directed at him, when listening to books you read him—and even when he overhears conversations around him, the more he will make the connection between sounds, words, things, and ideas. Unable to say, "Yes, I know what you're saying," he uses actions to let you know he's in on the game. Keep the game going by giving him opportunities to partake in your conversations. When you're giving him a bath, for instance, talk to him about what you're doing: "I'm washing your foot. Can you touch your foot?" If you direct his attention to his foot and congratulate him for touching it (even if he randomly happens upon it), you're helping him add words to his personal word bank. When reading, if you stop and say, "Can you pat the bunny?" he'll know by your inflection that you're asking for a response and he'll gladly provide one. To help him along, you can point to the bunny, saying, "I'm patting the bunny. Now it's your turn." Guide his hand and show him your delight when he makes

contact. When introducing new words, speak simply, keeping your sentences short and using emphasis to highlight meaning: "Here's your *spoon*. Hold your *spoon*."

Speak slowly and clearly to your toddler. Use key words in a variety of different ways. For example, if you point out a dog, you might say, "Do you see the furry dog in the yard? The dog is brown. The dog is barking."

Ideas are a bit harder for your child to grasp, but with repetition and experience, your child learns concept words, too. You can introduce words that describe feelings when your child is demonstrating various emotions: "You look *happy*." "Are you *hungry?*" "You're *sad* that your friend took your toy." Words that have opposite meanings are particularly interesting to your child: "The water is *cold*." "Don't touch! That's *hot!*" When your child gestures to be picked up or let down, respond in words as well as actions. "Do you want to be picked *up?*" "You want to get *down,* don't you?" Work with your child's natural desire to handle objects, describing qualities of things as he holds them. "This doll is *soft*." "The truck is *hard*." "The blanket is *fuzzy*."

Singing songs to your child is another way to expose him to the pleasures of hearing words. In addition to bedtime lullabies, include in your repertoire active songs that have gestures, such as "The Itsy-Bitsy Spider." Don't be surprised if your child comes to you and makes the hand gestures that accompany the song as his way of telling you he wants you to sing to him.

Speaking skills

As your child moves from making random sounds and happening upon words to consciously trying to form words, you may be tempted to step in and offer more help than he wants. It's best, however, to avoid focusing on pronunciation this year, relying instead on learning to decipher your child's jargoning. Look for clues in his gestures to alert you to what he's trying to say. If you're baffled by his meaning, don't try too hard to get him to explain himself unless he's indicating that he really needs you to understand his words. Most of the time, your toddler will be delighted when you simply acknowledge that he's talking to you and you talk to him in turn. Respond to let him know you heard him even if you don't understand what he said. It's okay to say, "I'm not sure what you want. Can you show me?" which can unlock the meaning by reassuring him that you want to know what he is saying. It's better to avoid saying things like, "I can't understand you," or, "I don't know what you're saying," which does not give him the sense that you are willing to try and would likely upset him. After all, he knows what you're saying and as far as he's concerned, he's speaking your language. Try not to let any frustration show on your part. Your role now is to be an appreciative audience for his speech making, not a reporter who needs to get all the facts straight.

To encourage him to make words, look for times you can ask questions. When reading to your child, you might pause and ask about a picture. When going out, you might stop and ask about sights and sounds that are new to him. Offer choices, such as asking whether he wants cereal or toast for breakfast. However, if your child does not answer in words, don't insist that he try. Work at understanding your child's baby talk, but don't mimic what he says, which may just confuse him. Instead of directing language at your child, such as saying simply, "We're going to the store now," try to get a conversation going. For example, you might say, "We're going to the store. What do you think we'll see at the store?" Then give him a chance to answer.

Play games that emphasize communication. For example, use toy telephones to talk to each other. Play with puppets together. Make up stories as your child maneuvers his action figures—just be careful not to take over his play.

Let your child know that you're interested in talking with him, in real conversations, not just in the functional uses of speaking. Get down on his level to talk, making eye contact. Invite him into family conversations, asking at the dinner table, for instance, "Do you like your mashed potatoes?" When there are others in a situation who are talkers—grown-ups and older kids—it's easy to forget that your toddler might want to be part of the conversation swirling around him. When people direct questions at him, give him a chance to respond for himself, rather than rushing in and saying something for him. For instance, if a neighbor comments on his cute hat, encourage him to respond, saying something like, "Can you show her the doggie on your hat?"

When your child says a word you understand, react positively. But don't overdo the praise. Too much adulation may cause him to shut down if he feels overwhelmed. To let your child know that you understand what he's saying, repeat what he says in different words. For instance, when he says, "Down bear," you can respond, "Oh, you want me to get the bear down from the shelf." If your child uses toddler syntax, saying, "Mommy and me go," don't directly correct him. Instead, demonstrate correct usage by noting that you understand his meaning: "Yes, you and I are going out."

Don't laugh or otherwise overreact when he mispronounces a word or happens to say an inappropriate word. He's too young to know that certain words are off-limits, and you don't want to encourage repetition of any accidental vulgarity by making too much of it. If you find something your toddler says especially amusing, write it down so you can share it with him when he is older.

Remember to give your child quiet time too, so that he can observe his environment and listen to himself talk and use sounds without an ongoing commentary.

Socializing with language

Like all other social skills—such as learning to share, acting politely, being honest—your child will look to you for cues on how to handle himself socially with language. During his toddler years, your child is ripe for learning the pleasures that conversing and social interactions bring. When you're out with him for a walk, and you encourage him to add his own "hi" when you meet a neighbor, you help him enlarge his social world beyond his family. When you say "please" and "thank you" to him as well as to others, he learns the social niceties that will serve him as he grows. Don't insist, however, that your child use these words regularly just yet. Even if he's able to pronounce "please," and fails to say it when he's asking for something, simply say, "I like it when you say please." Then provide the item he asked for if you would have done so anyway.

If your child...	Do say	Don't say
overgeneralizes, for example, calling every cat he sees by the name of his cat	"Yes, that's a cat like our Sasha!"	"That's not our Sasha. That's a cat."
points to his nose and says, "Nose"	"That's right. That's your nose."	"Now show me your ear. Say 'ear.'"
points to a bird, but doesn't name it	"You see the bird. What is the bird doing?"	"That's a bird. Say 'bird.'"
says "mi" to mean "milk"	"Do you want milk?"	"Say 'miLK'"
says "cow" when pointing to a horse	"That horse is big like a cow."	"That's a horse, not a cow."
says "Me out"	"You and I are going out."	"You mean that 'we're going out.'"

Using nursery rhymes

When learning to talk, your child, like most toddlers, probably loves the rhythm of speech and repetition of words. Nursery rhymes are perfect for entertaining him, and they have the added benefit of encouraging language development and social skills. While your child listens to the flow of the words, he also gets a great sense of vocabulary.

The best rhymes are those that also invite participation because they involve the body as well as the voice. For example, Pat-a-cake gives your child a chance to join in the rhythm, listen for the rhyme, and physically interact with you. "London Bridge," "This little piggy," "This is the way the lady rides," and "Ring-around-a-rosy" are other physical rhymes you can enjoy with your child and he can enjoy with other children.

In addition to one-on-one play, nursery rhymes can also provide comfort when your child is nervous or scared about something. Their reassuring predictability can make otherwise new experiences feel more familiar. Rhymes can transfix a child as he listens for the anticipated words and can thus make great additions to his everyday routines, slowing him down, calming him, and engaging him while you ready him for the bath, change his diaper, or place him in his car seat.

One way to reinforce the rhymes your child hears and enjoys is to read books that illustrate your child's favorite rhymes. This will be a great introduction to reading and will help your toddler make the connection between the words he loves to hear and pictures.

Reading to your child

Reading to your child fosters a love of language and of books. It's never too early to introduce a regular reading routine. The intimacy of the experience offers emotional comfort, and books can introduce your child to words and concepts that are not likely to be a part of his everyday life. Even if your child doesn't seem to express a lot of interest in reading time at first (perhaps because he is so busy mastering how to walk), you will find a growing interest over the year if you make this time a regular part of your day.

At first, your child will probably be more interested in the pictures than the story. He may want you to name and talk about the characters and objects he sees. At some point, he will become more interested in the story. Then he will want you to read it over and over, exactly the same way every time. Books that are themselves repetitive, containing rhymes and steady rhythms, will have particular appeal.

Because you know better than anyone what interests your toddler, you can take some freedoms with the text in order to make the story something your toddler will want to hear. You might shorten long passages, state ideas in simpler words, and completely leave out explanations and long descriptions. However, if your child has already come to know and love the unabridged version of a story, he's not likely to be content with your editing.

As you read, interact with your child by pointing to the pictures on each page. You might ask him to point to various objects within a picture, such as identifying the cow in a barnyard scene. If you are reading a book that's new to your child, introduce the new characters, objects, ideas, and colors. When you read the book again, you can ask your child to find familiar characters and objects. Don't be afraid to be dramatic in your performance of a story, using expression and gestures to make it more interesting and fun. Expression will also help your child learn some of the variations of language and speech and will help him understand a story even if he cannot understand the words.

Even though you may feel a little bored after reading the same story or rhyme three times in a row, your child will love the story each time, especially if the text rhymes. And you may find after several repetitions that he has memorized many of the rhyming words. Keep the stories and the reading times brief to help keep your child from growing restless and wandering off. You may find that his interest in story time will vary from day to day. He may sit happily and listen for several minutes, while on another day he is ready for a different activity in just a few seconds. Stop when he's ready to stop.

Set a good example to your child by showing your child that you are a reader, too. Even if you have very little time for reading, or don't particularly like to read, make sure that your toddler sees you read at least occasionally. Make sure that books and reading material are a part of your home. You might have a book by your bed, magazines on a coffee table in the living room, and a newspaper on the kitchen table every morning.

Books for toddlers

When choosing books for your child, include board books whose pages can't easily be torn, so that he can enjoy handling books himself. Let him look at pictures, turn pages, and even stack his books, rather than restricting book experiences to sitting quietly in your lap as you read. Books that invite interaction through touch-and-feel, looking for surprises under flaps, and so on will keep your child attentive, though these are best saved for times you're handling the book, since flap books can be dismantled easily. Vinyl books are also fun for the bathtub. (Make sure you dry them completely, however, so that mildew doesn't form on the pages.) Cloth books are usually not a good choice, as many children seem to feel they aren't the real thing and so ignore them. Save the more delicate paper books for times you read together.

Choose books that have big illustrations with bright colors. Your child will be drawn to pictures of familiar objects, babies, and animals. Also make sure that the text is simple. Alphabet books are fun for this age, not because your child is ready to learn the alphabet, but because they usually have simple, colorful pictures, with short text (often just one or two words per page).

Your local children's librarian or bookstore representative can be a great source of help in choosing books for your toddler. These classics are among those you might consider for your child:

◆ *All Fall Down* by Helen Oxenbury (Little Simon, 1999). This large-format board book pictures babies in a riot of activity that your toddler will enjoy and may want to imitate.

◆ *A to Z* by Sandra Boynton (Little Simon, 1995). This board book offers a funny look at the alphabet illustrated with silly animals. Other board books by Boynton include *Moo, Baa, La La La!* (Little Simon, 1995); *Doggies* (Little Simon, 1995); *Blue Hat, Green Hat* (Little Simon, 1995); *Opposites* (Little Simon, 1995); *But Not the Hippopotamus* (Little Simon, 1995); *Horns to Toes and In Between* (Little Simon, 1995); *The Going to Bed Book* (Little Simon, 1995); and *The Barnyard Dance* (Workman Publishing Co., 1993).

◆ *The Baby's Bedtime Book* by Kay Chorao (Puffin, 1994). This collection of classic poems and songs is part of a series that includes *The Baby's Lap Book* (Puffin, 1998) and *The Baby's Story Book* (E. P. Dutton, 1985).

◆ *Brown Bear, Brown Bear, What Do You See?* by Bill Martin, Jr. (Holt, 1967). This book includes color words and animal words in a text that encourages your child to join in.

◆ *The Cat in the Hat* by Dr. Seuss (Random House, 1956). Children never seem to tire of hearing about the Cat in the Hat's rainy afternoon visit. Other popular Seuss books for toddlers are *One Fish Two Fish Red Fish Blue Fish* (Random House, 1960), which includes verses about creatures at play and rest, and *Green Eggs and Ham* (Random House, 1960), in which the narrator insists he does not like green eggs and ham until he tastes them.

◆ *Finger Rhymes* by Marc Brown (Puffin, 1996). These rhymes and games will keep everyone laughing. Companion volumes are *Hand Rhymes* (Puffin, 1993) and *Party Rhymes* (Puffin, 1994).

♦ *Goodnight Moon* by Margaret Wise Brown (Harper & Row/ HarperCollins, 1947). This popular bedtime story features a bunny in pajamas who says goodnight to everything he sees before going to bed. This book is available as a board book, a storybook, and a pop-up.

♦ *The Little Duck* by Judy Dunn (Random House, 1976). This book is one in a series of photo-essays about small animals. The story is about a year in a duck's life as he is hatched and raised by a small boy. Other titles include *The Little Kitten* (Random House, 1983); *The Little Lamb* (Random House, 1977); *The Little Puppy* (Random House, 1984); and *The Little Rabbit* (Random House, 1980).

♦ *The Maggie B* by Irene Haas (Aladdin, 1975). In this fantasy, Margaret Barnstable dreams of being aboard the ship the *Maggie B* with her little brother, James. You can substitute the names of siblings when reading the story aloud.

♦ *Mother Goose: A Collection of Classic Nursery Rhymes* by Michael Hague (Henry Holt, 1988). In this collection, you'll find all your favorite rhymes to share with your child. You might also try *The Random House Book of Mother Goose* by Arnold Lobel (Random House, 1986). This collection includes 306 verses and is appropriate for all ages.

♦ *My Red Umbrella* by Robert Bright (Morrow, 1985). This small book tells the story of a little girl whose red umbrella grows bigger and bigger in a rain shower to shelter many different kinds of animals.

♦ *The Napping House* by Audrey Wood (Harcourt, 1983). In this funny tale, a child, a cat, a dog, and more find their way to Granny's bed, where they all sleep in a cozy heap.

♦ *Pat the Bunny* by Dorothy Kunhardt (Golden Books, 1990). This is an all-time favorite texture book in which your child can pat the bunny, feel Daddy's scratchy face, look in the mirror, and put a finger through Mommy's ring.

♦ *Richard Scarry's Best Little Word Book Ever* by Richard Scarry (Golden Books, 1997). You might find the pages crowded with too many details, jokes, and creatures, but your child will find them endlessly amusing.

♦ *Roar and More* by Karla Kuskin (Harper & Row/HarperCollins, 1990). Short, funny verses about animals introduce animals and their sounds.

♦ *Rotten Ralph* by Jack Gantos (Houghton Mifflin, 1976). This is the first story in a series about a very bad cat named Ralph. Your child will enjoy hearing about all the bad things Rotten Ralph gets into.

♦ *The Runaway Bunny* by Margaret Wise Brown (Harper & Row/HarperCollins, 1972). The little bunny in this story plays hide-and-seek, knowing that mother will always be able to find him no matter where he is. Your child will have fun finding the bunny in the garden, on the mountain, and at the circus.

♦ *The Very Hungry Caterpillar* by Eric Carle (Putnam, 1984). A caterpillar eats his way through different foods until he becomes a butterfly. Look for this book in its original hardcover edition; with its large format and stiff pages, your child can easily poke his fingers through the holes in the apple, pear, strawberry, and other foods.

♦ *When You Were a Baby* by Ann Jonas (Greenwillow, 1982). Discovering some things a toddler can do now, but couldn't do as a baby, is a sure hit with toddlers, and bound to make them proud.

Some other classic stories that are available as board books for younger children include:

♦ *Good Dog, Carl* by Alexandra Day (Little Simon, 1996).

♦ *Humpty Dumpty and Other Rhymes,* edited by Iona Archibald Opie (Candlewick Press, 1997).

♦ *More, More, More Said the Baby* by Vera B. Williams (Tupelo Books, 1997).

♦ *Snoozers' 7 Short Bedtime Stories for Lively Little Kids* by Sandra Boynton (Little Simon, 1997).

♦ *The Snowy Day* by Ezra Jack Keats (Viking, 1996).

In addition to storybooks, wordless picture books can also be fun as they encourage inventing your own stories to go along with the pictures. Here are a few classic examples:

♦ *Changes, Changes* by Pat Hutchins (Aladdin Paperbacks, 1987). This classic wordless book follows the changes of two wooden figures and blocks that turn into a boat, a wagon, and a house.

♦ *Is It Red? Is It Yellow? Is It Blue?* by Tana Hoban (Greenwillow, 1978). This book shows primary colors in photographs of everyday objects. Other titles for toddlers by Hoban include *Shapes, Shapes, Shapes* (Mulberry Books, 1996); *A Children's Zoo* (Greenwillow, 1985); *Is It Rough? Is It Smooth? Is It Shiny?* (Greenwillow, 1984); and *I Read Signs* (William Morrow & Co. Paper, 1987).

♦ *The Snowman* by Raymond Briggs (Random House, 1989). The pictures tell the story of a snowman that comes to life in the dreams of the boy who made him. The video version is also a total delight.

Recordings for toddlers

Your child may also enjoy hearing and learning songs geared especially for toddlers. Following are some suggestions for appropriate recordings:

♦ *Babes, Beasts, and Birds* by Pat Carfa (Lullaby Lady Records, distributed by Alcazar). These recordings include a collection of lullabies and greet-the-day songs from different countries.

♦ *Baby's Nursery Rhymes* from the Stories to Remember series (Lightyear Entertainment, 1995). Actress Phylicia Rashad reads traditional Mother Goose rhymes to a jazzy musical score by Jason Miles. There is also a video version.

♦ *Hello Everybody!* by Rachel Buchman (A Gentle Wind, 1998). A mix of original songs and familiar tunes gives your child a great collection of rhymes, lullabies, and play-along songs.

♦ *Sleepytime Serenade* by Linda Schrade (Gentle Wind Audio, 1989). Schrade invites singing along with a variety of songs accompanied by guitar and flute.

The importance of being me

Your toddler's personality

Before your toddler was born, you probably imagined in great detail just who she would be and what she might be like. Whom would she take after? Would she be easygoing like you were as a child? Rambunctious like your siblings? Someone who loved to read like your spouse? An athlete? A born adventurer? No matter who she was, you were sure that you would be able to understand what made her tick. After all, she would have your influence to guide her.

When your child begins growing into her own person, you may be surprised to discover that she is different from you, and perhaps different from other members of the family, too. If you are outgoing, your toddler's quiet demeanor may come as a surprise to you. If you're a little uncomfortable in unfamiliar situations, you may be amazed that your child enjoys new experiences, literally jumping into any new situation. As many parents do, you might ask yourself, "Who is this little person?" On the other hand, you and your child may share many personality traits, see the world from a similar perspective, and have the same range of reactions to different experiences.

DEVELOPMENTAL MILESTONE
The emergence of personality
Even in your child's infancy, you saw clues that gave you insight into her nature. The manner in which your child reacts spontaneously to her environment is her inborn temperament. The mingling of her temperament with her interactions with the environment around her results in her behavior, or personality.

While temperament is determined by her genes and will not change radically over her lifetime, her behavior can change from year to year, month to month, and even minute to minute. Her experiences and her relationship to others, and even how she's feeling physically and emotionally, determine how her temperament is expressed. The naturally shy child who is patiently guided to join in with others, who finds herself welcomed by new friends, and who is well rested and fed, may, despite her natural shyness, be socially comfortable. Likewise, a naturally aggressive child who has been taught to control her impulses and has learned to approach others in a more cooperative manner may be regarded as relatively easygoing.

Your one-year-old's responses to her surroundings now may be consistent with her personality as an infant. For example, she may have been distracted easily by motion and activity as a baby and still is. She may have been an active infant and is now an active toddler. In contrast, it is also possible that the responses your child exhibits to her surroundings now may be quite different from the way she acted when she was an infant. This would be because the interaction of her temperament with her environment could yield a new personality. If she was an easygoing, unflappable baby, she may now be anxious or shy in new situations. If she reacted to noise and activity in a sensitive way as an infant, she may now race toward action with great confidence, eager to participate.

To understand how temperament affects personality and behavior, it helps to look at the traits that determine temperament.

Traits that determine temperament
In 1956, psychiatrists Dr. Stella Chess and Dr. Alexander Thomas began a study in which they followed 136 children from birth through young adulthood. During this time, as they studied the children's behavior, they were able to isolate nine categories, such as adaptability and intensity, that could be measured along a continuum. Chess and Thomas determined that all nine traits are present to some degree in every child.

Intensity. This category reflects the level of a child's responses to her surroundings when she is upset, hungry, tired, or happy. For example, when happy, she may show a moderate level of intensity by smiling, or she may show a high level of intensity by squealing with delight.

Activity. You can measure a child's activity level by observing if she remains fairly still when you diaper or bathe her—a low activity level; or, if she consistently tries to wiggle away from you—a high activity level. The child with a low activity level may be content to sit on your lap for an extended period of time, while the child with a high activity level will want to move on to another activity after a brief hug.

Sensitivity. The degree of stimulation such as noise, light, sights, and texture that a child responds to reflects her sensitivity level. If a child complains that her clothing itches, perceives differences in flavors and textures of foods, easily notices if you or another family member changes his or her appearance such as after a haircut, then your child exhibits a high degree of sensitivity. Sensitive children may also be easily startled by loud noises, react strongly to bright lights, and may be upset by a lot of activity and motion around them. A child with low sensitivity may not be aware of important physical sensations such as being overheated or needing her diaper changed.

Mood. This category reflects how a child generally seems to feel about the world. Moods may range from pleasant responses, with lots of smiles and laughs, to a more somber, quiet manner, or fussy behavior with lots of whining.

Regularity. If a child's bodily functions are predictable, then she has a set rhythm, or is regular. For example, a regular child may get hungry at about the same time every day, eat the same amount of food, become tired at the same time, sleep the same number of hours every night, wake at the same time every morning, and need a diaper change at consistent intervals. A regular child may react strongly to any change in her routine. A child who is not regular is less predictable; you may have to guess when she is hungry, and her waking and sleeping times may vary from day to day. She's less likely to be thrown off by changes in her routine.

Initial reaction. This measures how a child first reacts to new people, experiences, foods, and routines. Some children crave newness and respond positively to the unknown. Others hold back and are generally more cautious.

Adaptability. Following a child's initial reaction to a new experience, her adaptability level is measured by how quickly she adjusts to something new. Her adaptability is on the low side if she continues to hold back or if she has difficulty stopping a behavior even after you have told her to do so more than once. An adaptable child warms up to a new experience, even if her initial reactions are cautious. She isn't likely to insist on continuing to do something you have asked her to stop, especially if you provide her with a distraction.

Distractibility. A toddler, by virtue of her age, is more distractible than children of other ages. As she grows, she will become less distractible through maturity and perhaps a conscious effort not to be. However, a child with a highly distractible temperament will always be more easily sidetracked by interruptions and less able to pick up an activity where she left off than a child of the same age with low distractability. If she is able to continue with an activity, even when there are other things going on around her, then she has low distractibility.

Persistence. The length of time your child can stick with a single activity reflects her persistence level. A highly persistent child may continue playing with a door handle until she figures out how to open it. If she quickly moves on to something else after a first attempt fails, then she has low persistence. A child may be distractible and persistent at the same time if she is able to go back to and pick up an activity from which she was sidetracked once the distraction has passed. A child with a high level of persistence reacts strongly to being interrupted from an activity she enjoys. If a child has low persistence, she may find it difficult to finish projects when she gets older and will need help breaking down tasks into short steps.

Temperament types

These nine traits combine in different ways to form your child's temperament. Chess and Thomas determined that all the various combinations of traits produced temperaments that fell into three broad categories—easy, slow to warm up, and difficult. Further research added a fourth category—active—to their list and re-phrased *difficult* as *challenging*. Within these four categories can be found some or all of the traits described by Chess and Thomas in varying degrees. For example, while a high level of some traits produces an active child, a low level of the same traits would result in an easy child. These four categories can be helpful in under-standing individual children, but it's important to resist applying any label to your child with too strong an adhesive. Children's behavior changes as they grow and their experiences enhance or tone down their natural tendencies. These four categories can help, however, in determining the best methods of responding to your child's behavior.

Easy. If your child has an easy temperament, she is usually in a good mood, quick to smile, and adapts readily to change. She enjoys new situations and rarely exhibits intense or exaggerated emotions. She has no problem following a routine, but is also will-ing to be spontaneous. When she complains, she often does so in a quiet and reasonable manner. The challenge in raising an easy child is to remain alert to her needs. An easy child may need to learn to assert herself and to recognize and argue for her own wants rather than comply with others too readily.

Slow to warm up. If your child is slow to warm up, she takes a long time to ease into a new situation. If given an opportunity to observe quietly from a distance, she will join in eventually with as much eagerness as other children once she has examined the situ-ation and feels ready to participate. If rushed, she will react strongly. She may then resist leaving this same situation as fierce-ly as she resisted entering it. Because she takes so long to assess a situation, you may consider your slow-to-warm-up child shy and timid, or even anxious. In general, she may not be active or express emotions in an extreme manner. The challenge in raising a slow-to-warm-up-child is recognizing that she'll always require extra patience and special guidance to become part of social situations. She'll also need help learning how to make transitions from one activity to another.

Challenging. If your child constantly challenges you and others, you may describe her as demanding and stubborn, or assertive and high-spirited, depending on your own assessment of her tempera-ment. She may be unable to establish any regular routine, be sen-sitive to too much activity, and have trouble adapting to change. She might also wake up in a bad mood, be difficult to please, and express intense emotions in an exaggerated and extreme manner, such as shrieking, screaming, and crying in response to various situations. She may resist direction and be easily overstimulated. Raising a challenging child requires more—more patience, more consistency, more energy—than raising most other children. You'll have to be careful to choose clothing that's comfortable, keep stim-ulation such as bright lights and loud noises to a minimum within the home, and maintain routines designed to reduce confronta-tions. You'll need lots of patience in handling your child's extreme moods. Discipline will have to be particularly consistent, as will making a point of showing positive, loving responses to your child and being available for her displays of affection.

Active. Runs rather than walks? Climbs on chairs? Can't stand still? Is fearless? Loves to take risks? If this describes your child, she is an active toddler. Such high energy can be exhausting for nonactive parents, but exciting if you yourself like to keep on the move. Keeping your active child safe is a challenge, as she probably seems determined to try every dangerous thing she can imagine. She also may not display the usual signs of fatigue when she's tired, so you need to make sure she gets enough rest, even if she doesn't seem ready to slow down.

All of these temperament types have their positive and negative sides, but no one kind of temperament is good or bad. Some, however, tend to be viewed more positively or negatively. For example, grown-ups and other children are more drawn to a happy, cheerful child than to one who whines and frequently complains. An intense child who has tantrums after being told "No" is much more of a challenge than a less intense child who reacts more mildly. However, when understood, each kind of temperament can be seen as positive when you learn to work with your child's temperament rather than against it. Whatever traits are naturally present can also be modified so that your child can behave in socially acceptable ways without having to suppress her own nature.

CONFLICT
Your response to your child's temperament

Your child is anxious to please you, yet at the same time, she is driven to be herself. Her ability to win your approval, therefore, is largely determined by your response to her temperament and behavior. Do you see your demanding baby as delightfully assertive or as hard to manage? Are you content to join your easygoing baby in quiet games or do you try to prod her into being just a bit more active? Does your active toddler strike you as exuberant or exhausting?

Walking and talking, which are skills your child acquires over time following certain predictable stages, easily win your approval because you accept that these developments are normal and expected. Certainly these new skills present challenges for both of you, but you don't try to interfere with their forward movement. A first step or a first word is celebrated. Both of you are aware that these new skills are positive accomplishments. Her goal—and yours—is that she become more mobile, more communicative, more like you.

But accepting your child's natural behavior is far more subjective; you may not always be sure how to respond to her tendencies. You may want her to be more like you, but that may be impossible for her. On the other hand, you may prefer to weed out those traits of yours that you don't like if you see them emerging in her. That effort is also futile.

The conflict arises for your child when you correct her or show that you disapprove of who she is. For a toddler, such disapproval is especially confusing because it comes at a time when she's just beginning to realize that she is a separate and unique individual.

As she matures, you can help her learn to integrate her natural tendencies with the needs of those around her, learning, for example,

How it feels to be me

Children of each temperament type respond in their own distinct manners to a situation such as a visit to the playground. Here's how each might feel:

Easy. I think this will be fun. I see other children to play with. I see colors and movements that interest me. I'm glad to be here. When another child approaches me, I show her my sandbox toy. I smile to let her know that I want to be friends. I like the feeling of the sand on my hands. When another child takes my toy, I don't really know what to do. Can I get it back? I'll wait and see. Maybe if I hand him his own toy he'll give me mine back. Or I'll play with his for now. I'm okay in the sandbox because I can see Mommy. Stay near in case I want to spend some time with you. And, please don't have me play in the sandbox all afternoon even though I seem to be just fine here. There are other things I'd like to see and do.

Slow-to-warm-up. There's so much going on here. I'll stay in your lap for now because I'm not at all sure I want to be here. I notice another child playing with a truck. It looks interesting, but I can see it fine from here. When the truck owner pushes his truck closer to me, I need to hide in your arms. He's moving in faster than I want him to. Now that I've to sit relatively quietly at the table in a restaurant or in the class-room without feeling that she is being denied her own personality and will never be allowed to run around. Now, however, your best bet is to limit the situations in which your child needs to behave in ways that are antithetical to her personality. If your toddler cannot sit still in a restaurant, avoid taking her to restaurants for the time being. If crowds frighten her, don't take her into large social groups, or, at the very least, stay with her at a party so she will feel safe even if other toddler guests appear to be enjoying socializing. What's important now for your child's sense of emotional comfort is for her to know that who she is is who she should be, and that you are supportive of her—personality quirks and all.

watched him for a while, I feel safe enough to walk over to him. Maybe I'll even sit down next to him and play. This is not the time to leave or to try to interest me in the slide. I'm still checking out the child with the truck.

Challenging. My shirt is scratchy and I can't concentrate on anything else. I'm tired. I want to play. Let me go. I want to touch that truck I see. I'm happy because the truck is really fun to touch. I'm sad and angry because the other child is playing with the truck. I want it. My shirt is scratchy. When you put me on the swing, it feels great. I'm so happy I could scream. I want to go higher. I love this. I want to stop and do something else now. You might think I'm crying because the swing scared me. I just want to play in the sandbox now. The sand sticks to my hands. I don't like that at all.

Active. First the slide, then the sandbox, then the swings. There's so much to do. I see a bench to climb and a gate to open. I can run the whole length of the playground and never get tired. I like it when you chase after me. There's a pebble on the ground. I wonder how far I can throw it. The slide has a ladder I can climb. I can do it over and over again. I won't wait for you to help me climb the ladder. I want to do it now. I can't stand to wait for anything.

To help your child learn to accept her own unique temperament and feel good about herself, avoid labeling her or allowing others to do so when her behavior clashes with expectations. It's important to remember that even though particular traits may dominate her temperament, your child is complex, with many facets to her personality.

If your child...	Do say	Don't say
hesitates approaching another child in a playgroup	"It looks to me like you need me to stay close to you for a moment."	"Don't be so shy. Go over and play."
zooms from one activity to another at the playground	"Show me what you like to do on the slide," to focus her attention for the moment on the activity in which she is engaged.	"You're so wild. Slow down!"
pushes you away when she's in an angry mood	"I see you're angry. Let me help you calm down," and then hold her closely or otherwise comfort her.	"Bad girl. Never push me."
happily plays by herself with a new toy	"I see you're playing. Would you like me to join you?"	"Let me show you how that works."

Working with your child's temperament

Piecing together the puzzle of your child's temperament is not complete without examining one very important piece—you. Your response to your child's temperament is a key to how her personality will emerge. When her temperament is well matched to yours, you naturally understand her better; her behavior, likes, and dislikes make sense to you. However, when you have similar temperaments, there is also the danger that you may overlook the differences that do exist between you and miss opportunities to encourage your child's individual interests and potential.

Differences in your natural responses to the world, of course, also complicate your relationship with one another. If you struggle to remake your child's temperament into something more like your own, you'll both be frustrated and unhappy. As long as you remain sensitive to your child's inherent disposition, the rhythm of your life with your child in your everyday routines can proceed in a mutually beneficial way. You'll know, for instance, to keep a particularly watchful eye on your active toddler, not to overstimulate your challenging child, to be patient with your slow-to-warm-up child, or to pay special attention to your easy child's needs.

Through an understanding of your child's temperament and your own, you can find ways that the two of you can work well together. This doesn't mean that you will eliminate conflict. It does mean that you will be more willing to look for compromises that you both can live with. Start by evaluating your own temperament. Review the descriptions of traits and temperament types. Do any of these fit with how you remember yourself as a child, or how family members remember you? Which descriptions still apply? Next, consider whether you have negative feelings about any of the traits you have identified in your own temperament. If there are parts of your temperament that you are dissatisfied with, you may project these criticisms onto your own child if she displays any of the same traits.

Think about what you have learned about your child. How do you think your own temperament might color your perception of how your child behaves? For example, you might perceive your child's whining as evidence that she is difficult. Another parent may see this same behavior as assertive. Still another may simply see the whining as a reaction to a particular circumstance and work to correct the reasons for the whining rather than just correcting the child.

It's always important to remember that even though your child's temperament will not change radically over time, the way her temperament manifests itself will change as she matures. With your guidance, the easy child may learn to demand the attention she needs. The active child can learn to control her runaway impulses. The challenging child, given the help she needs, will temper her reactions and behave in socially acceptable ways. The slow-to-warm-up child, once she has more social experiences under her belt, will be less reticent. Moreover, your influence on the qualities that your child develops as she grows—kindness, honesty, tolerance, responsibility—will ultimately form her character and will serve as the basis for your relationship with her and her relationship with the world.

HELPING YOUR CHILD GROW
Bringing out the best in your child's personality

Trying to change your child's personality is like trying to mold something into a shape that just won't hold. You may be able to achieve some compliance by promoting behavior that is opposed to her nature, but it will be short-lived. This doesn't mean that you should approve misbehavior or allow your child to act in ways that are dangerous to herself or others. Rather, it means guiding her in learning strategies to help her use her temperamental strengths to her advantage, while learning how to control the weaknesses. Having the patience and the awareness to help your child learn to handle her own temperament can be hard, especially if there are aspects of it that you find difficult to deal with. But the rewards of doing so are great; your child will grow up with her self-esteem intact, which is essential to forging a strong relationship with you and others. Here are some suggestions for helping your child make the most of her temperament:

Your easy child

Your easy child's flexible disposition presents fewer challenges than children of other temperaments. Learn to tune into her emotional needs, even though she may not share her feelings readily by—for example—angry tantrums or gleeful twirls around the kitchen just for the joy of it. You'll have to look closely to know how she's feeling. She can grow as scared or upset about some things as less adaptable children, but she may not show it as readily. Parents of easy children also need to remember not to set behavioral expectations too high. Your easy child's willingness to be agreeable can lead you to believe that she is more mature and capable than she really is.

With an easy child, your options for toys, activities, and routines probably seem limitless. Your toddler will be ready to try anything new and to have fun doing so. While her easy temperament makes her a pleasure to care for, she, like all children, needs specific things.

Don't overload her with new experiences. Even though she seems to accept any and all transitions, your easy child needs time to explore activities and objects and to set her own pace for moving forward, like other children. Now that she's beginning to talk, you may be anxious to share as much as possible with her, but exposing her to too much can be confusing and tiring and may dull, rather than heighten, her interest. Be sure to include plenty of rest times and opportunities to regress, such as leaving her alone to play with a rattle that she "outgrew" months ago. A brief regression is often a child's reaction to learning too much too fast. It's her way of slowing down for a while to give herself an opportunity to absorb what she has learned before she moves on to something new.

Choose new toys that are somewhat challenging but still age-appropriate. She may be willing to try anything, but may grow frustrated if a toy is too complicated or an activity is too far beyond her abilities. Allow her the pleasure of revisiting old toys and activities.

Expect her to share much of what she discovers with you. She'll hand you anything new she finds so that you, too, can enjoy looking at it. Your easy toddler takes particular delight in spending time with you, showing off what she can do, and sharing the good times. Be sure to acknowledge the fun and show excitement over her discoveries, rather than simply appreciating her ability to entertain herself.

When she's troubled by something, help her find the words to express herself. For instance, say, "I see that the dog is frightening you. Would you like me to hold you?" Easy children may not shout or run away from something that troubles them and may need special attention when they're frightened.

Don't be too quick to rescue your child in all social situations. For example, if a child takes her toy in the sandbox, ask, "Would you like to have your toy back?" rather than swooping in to make everything okay. It may be fine with her that another child is sharing her toy. Or maybe it's not. Taking over in social situations undermines her ability to work things out for herself.

Your slow-to-warm-up child

Just because your child is slow to warm up, don't assume that she will approach every situation in a cautious, timid manner. Like other children, yours needs opportunities to mingle and develop social skills, so don't overprotect her from social situations. Your child does need your patience and the firm knowledge that she can go to you if she needs to. If you don't push, you will help relieve any anxiety she may feel over finding herself in the middle of something before she's ready.

You may be hesitant to put your child in day care because you know she would have a difficult time with strangers and new surroundings. While she may be upset at first, she will adjust better if you prepare her ahead of time. This might mean visiting a few times beforehand so that she can become familiar. During any period of transition, other routines at home should be kept as consistent as possible so that your child doesn't have to deal with too many new experiences at once. As long as you're prepared for this necessary warm-up period, which may involve holding her or letting her stay very close to you for several minutes, you may discover that your child is more than willing to take part in new situations.

It's important not to interpret every episode of holding back as evidence of your child's temperament. A shy stance could also indicate fear or displeasure. Now that your toddler can understand much of what you say, be sure to ask about situations and give her a chance to answer with a nod or otherwise. Without becoming overly protective, try to find ways to reduce your child's social anxiety.

Look for less active children who are a good match for your child. You might start a conversation with another toddler and then draw your child in. Give the children a chance to reach out to each other, rather than pushing them to interact.

Accompany your child into a new situation. Observe together what is going on and talk about what you see. Allow her to watch the action from the safety of your arms, if that's what she wants. Remain nearby until you see that your child is beginning to get involved and enjoy an activity. Then retreat to where you won't be hovering, but can easily be called back if your child needs you. If your child does call you, determine how anxious she appears. If she is obviously upset, go to her. If she seems uncertain, you may only need to give a reassuring wave.

Adhere to routines and announce upcoming transitions.
This allows your child to be better prepared for the changes ahead. For example, if you are at the playground, you may want to tell your child that it will be time to go a few minutes before you actually have to leave. Tell her what you plan to do next. She may not be able to verbalize what's going on herself, but she will understand your end of the conversation.

When it's time to buy your child new clothing, try to find items that are similar to what she already wears. Differences in the feel of clothing can make her particularly uncomfortable.

Allow her to eat the same things every day if this makes her feel more secure. Vary the meals just enough to provide good nutrition. Every once in a while try introducing a new food or a new way to prepare a favorite food. For example, you might show her how to cut a piece of bread with a cookie cutter to make a fun, new shape. If she shows little interest in trying something new, don't push her. Wait a week or two before introducing the new item again. Eventually, she will begin to try new things.

Try role-playing with a teddy bear or a doll to help your child adapt to new situations. For example, you might say that the bear wants to play with the other toys but is not sure what to do. Ask your child to help the bear join the other toys.

Allow your toddler to follow her own interests. She may be most interested in revisiting the same toys and games over and over. Try not to show your frustration or to foist new activities on her too often.

When she chooses to enter a social situation, don't overpraise her. Just because she took the first step this time doesn't mean she's now ready to jump in with both feet. Continue to let her set the pace, while gently encouraging further involvement with others.

Your challenging child

It's tempting to call a challenging child "difficult" but it's important to view aspects of this personality in a more positive light. There are other words that might be better used and can help you more effectively nurture your child. Words such as *spirited, persistent, sensitive, strong-willed,* and *determined* also describe your child's temperament and carry much more positive connotations. If you view your child's personality in a more positive light, your pleasure in raising her will be amplified. Moreover, your pleasure will be reflected in her behavior, since knowing that she has you as an ally will soothe her tremendously. Becoming attuned to situations that trigger her outbursts will help you minimize difficult times. Choosing your battles wisely when disciplining will help ensure that you don't become locked in a battle of wills with your child. The structure of a routine will be a great help in gaining your child's cooperation.

One of the best ways you can help your challenging child is to make sure she knows that you're going to do whatever you can to help her deal with a world that often seems overwhelming and upsetting. Here are some suggestions for helping your child:

Stay calm yourself if your child becomes overexcited. You will only increase the tension and the problem by scolding her harshly. You may need to tell her that you will help her to calm down and may have to remove her physically from a situation in order to help her get a handle on her feelings. In this way, you acknowledge that she is probably unable to calm herself down, and, though she may initially appear not to want your help, she will be relieved to have you take over for a while.

If your child doesn't like to be touched, give her an opportunity to be alone. Some challenging children respond positively to being held tightly and lovingly, but others do not.

Try whispering. This way, she'll have to quiet down to hear you.

Talk about what you're going to do in advance of any activity. State rules and expectations as simply as possible. Your child may not remember everything you say, but reminders along the way will reinforce your message.

Observe the things your child does like and the way she approaches activities. Try to accommodate her preferences as much as possible without giving your child the sense that she is in charge. If one of her traits is persistence, make sure you allow enough time for her to explore and pursue an activity. When it comes time to move on, give her plenty of warning and gently ease her into the next activity.

Recognize your child's sensitivity. If she often complains of itchy clothing or being hot much of the time, acknowledge her concerns. Try to find a material that is less annoying to her. Make sure her clothes fit well and don't pinch or scratch. Pay attention to the patterns or colors that may bother her and avoid these when buying new clothes. If bright lights and loud noises tend to upset her, try to decrease the level of light and sound in your home. Turning off the TV or turning off electric lights in favor of daylight can go a long way toward soothing your child.

Accept that you may not be able to establish a predictable schedule if your toddler has difficulty sticking to a routine. For example, if she doesn't want to eat when it's dinnertime, offer a snack and save dinner for later. When it comes to bedtime, you could try varying the time slightly from night to night depending on your child's mood, but otherwise, as much as possible, maintain a soothing routine.

When it comes to playthings, let her follow her own interests.
As you may have already discovered, offering her things she hasn't chosen herself may upset her. You might put toys where she is able to find them in her own time and let her decide for herself what she wants to play with.

Your active child

All toddlers require a lot of supervision to prevent them from entering dangerous situations. Your active toddler doesn't have the maturity to control her hazardous impulses or the ability to understand and remember all of your warnings. She lives to move and do and go. Characteristically, she combines high intensity and a short attention span with her high activity level. Your job is to provide a secure base from which she can rush ahead and to be ready to pull her back when she goes too far. Here are some ideas for keeping her safe and happy:

Work hard to keep your child from becoming bored, which could lead her to explore beyond safe limits. Leave out only a few toys at a time to keep her from hopping from one to the next without fully exploring anything. Put some toys away and introduce them periodically to maintain her interest in these items.

Provide safe places to be active. For example, if your child regularly attempts to jump off the furniture, put a small mattress on the floor to soften her landing. You might also set up a safe place to climb, such as a low, soft chair, or the bottom two steps of a staircase after you block off the remaining steps.

Don't assume that your child is fearless. It's important to watch for signs of wariness and fright and be ready to help. Even a very active toddler may develop typical toddler fears, of the bath, for instance, and become intimidated by a new experience.

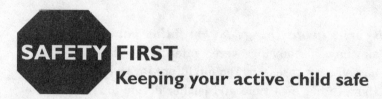

SAFETY FIRST
Keeping your active child safe

If your child has an active temperament, you have probably discovered that she often seems to be a daredevil. The couch may become a trampoline, the cabinets make a great ladder, and a table is a wonderful place for dancing. She may seem to have no sense of danger. Everything presents a chance to explore, and her trusting nature tells her that anything that interests her is okay to investigate.

So how can you keep your energetic child safe? While all parents of toddlers need to create a safe place for their children to run and climb, your challenge is multiplied. Install child-safe latches; you'll need them just about everywhere. Vary the layout of your toddler's safe space regularly so that she doesn't get bored and try to explore other locations. You might remove the sofa cushions one day and place them on the floor to provide a safe way to climb and to jump. Make an easy-to-reach cabinet a safe place to investigate by filling it with unbreakable items with different textures. These might include toys, soft balls, old placemats, and small pillows. Childproof the rest of your house, too, as you can depend on your child's reckless energy and high curiosity to get her into anything she can get into.

More than providing a safe place for whatever an active toddler wants to do, you will need to be

Don't put your active toddler in too many situations that require her to sit still for any period of time yet. Eventually she can learn to sit through an entire restaurant meal or be quiet during a wedding service, but for now it's best to find a good caregiver to be with her during times when you need to socialize.

Call on other children and siblings to play with your child. Also, don't hesitate to ask other adults to watch her for a while so you can get some time off.

especially watchful away from home. Carefully inspect any playground equipment to ensure that it is sturdy and appropriate for your child's age. Also check your child's clothing to make sure there are no hanging strings or other loose parts that might catch on playground equipment as she moves quickly from one activity to the next. After she enjoys climbing, jumping, and running in a safe place, she may want to continue these same activities in a place that is not safe.

You will have to impose limits on what your child can do, even if restrictions upset her. This doesn't mean making her sit still for extended periods of time. It does mean reining her in and redirecting her energies when she exceeds the limits you have set. For example, if your active toddler insists on squirming when you try to buckle her into the car seat, you should return her to the seat with as little upset and emotion as possible. When she does sit quietly in the seat for a time, pay more positive attention to her than you did when she was wriggling out of the seat.

If your child is especially wild and reckless, call on all the help you can get. If you are exhausted from trying to keep her out of danger, then you are less likely to remain watchful. Don't hesitate to ask your spouse, a relative, a friend, or a baby-sitter to assist you in watching and playing with your active toddler. If you can get even a short break, you will have more energy to deal with your child's adventurous nature.

Have distractions on hand. While you're involved in other things, such as cooking or talking on the phone, engage your child's interest. A portable phone that allows you to follow your child while you talk is a good investment. Place pots and pans, plastic containers, wooden spoons, and other safe objects within your child's reach while you're cooking. Noisy distractions have the added benefit of helping you keep an ear as well as an eye on your child, but they won't be of much help to you if you are trying to talk to someone on the phone.

Appreciate quiet times. Don't assume that just because she is active she doesn't like quiet times, too. If your child wants to cuddle, don't postpone it; the urge may not come again for a while. When your child is ready for a nap, try to take one yourself, too. Have puzzles, blocks, and stuffed toys on hand in addition to more active toys.

To help your active child slow down on occasion, try some of these relaxation techniques:

♦ Play quiet music

♦ Hug and cuddle

♦ Read a story

♦ Give your child a warm bath

♦ Offer crayons, paint, or clay to encourage some sitdown activity

♦ Engage your child in some supervised water play, perhaps showing her how to pour water from one plastic cup into another

Managing your toddler's playdates

Between the ages of one and two, your child may enjoy being with other children, but may not actually engage in play with them. Young toddlers are often happy with "parallel play," pursuing their own interests in the company of other children. Observing the other child is an educational and intriguing experience, but the give-and-take of playful interaction won't take place just yet.

Toddlers of any temperament usually can't sustain a long playdate, so limit it to an hour or so. If the playdate is indoors, invite only one other child. If you can go outdoors where there is more space, consider inviting more than one child. Schedule the play-date for a time when your child will be well rested and not hungry. Ask the other child's parent to bring some of his own toys, too.

When choosing playmates, it's best to consider your child's temperament as well as those of potential playmates. However, kids of any temperament can enjoy any other child's company with some help from you. Realize, of course, that you will remain the focus of your child's attention, even as she is intrigued by the presence of another child and, perhaps, the other child's toys.

To help prepare your child, talk about the playdate in advance. Tell her what you plan to do. When the child and parent arrive you may want to offer a snack. Then take out a toy or two of your child's and the playmate's and give each a chance to examine the other's goodies. Keep expectations for sharing and playing together to an absolute minimum and you won't be disappointed. Don't insist that they play together or trade toys. Be prepared to intervene only if they are harming one another, and, in that case, try not to overreact to signs of aggression on either child's part. This socializing is new to toddlers and, with practice, they will get the idea.

I am some body

Your toddler's sense of self

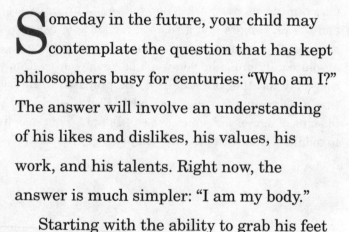

Someday in the future, your child may contemplate the question that has kept philosophers busy for centuries: "Who am I?" The answer will involve an understanding of his likes and dislikes, his values, his work, and his talents. Right now, the answer is much simpler: "I am my body."

Starting with the ability to grab his feet as an infant, your child has been discovering how his body feels, what parts it has, and the fact that it can feel hunger, pain, tiredness, cold, heat, and so many other physical sensations. He is learning that his body can walk and run, jump and climb, reach and bend, and even dance. He is also finding out that he is a separate individual, that other people are not him and he is not them. He begins to see what his physical boundaries are—where he ends and the world begins. To your child, his body is fascinating and wonderful, and therefore, he himself is fascinating and wonderful. His relationship with his body at this stage in his life lays the groundwork for how his sense of self, including his emotions and intellect, will develop.

DEVELOPMENTAL MILESTONE
Your child's self-awareness

Your toddler's sense of self is limited to his perception of himself as a physical being. That's not to say that he doesn't experience his emotions as real, but his sense of his emotions is tied to his physical wants and needs. For instance, if he feels sad or angry because you've restricted his ability to climb to the top of the bookcase, he experiences his feelings by physically struggling, thinking, "I can't get to where I want to be." When he delights in splashing in the tub, again it's the physically pleasurable sensations that he experiences as happiness.

As he begins to walk and reach and hold things with his hands, his body takes him into the world and helps him find fun and interesting things to explore. He is dependent on his senses to tell him about things, so his hands want to poke and touch, shake and bang. His hands bring things to his mouth, where he can find out how they taste and feel. As his teeth emerge, he may at times feel an irresistible urge to bite things and sometimes people because he wants to find out what it feels like. Biting, along with hitting and other physical acts, is also a way to express his impulses and frustration. Since his perception of the world is based on the physical, his responses are physical, too.

Learning what his body can do—and learning about the world in general—is a focus of his energies now. He loves looking at himself in the mirror, watching changes in his facial expressions and how movements that he controls are reflected back. Now that he has the power to get around by himself, he takes his body wherever it can go. He tries to see if he can fit into small spaces and climb into high ones. What his hands can do is truly awesome—picking up small items and placing them inside containers, touching every type of surface to see how it feels against his skin, bending objects, taking things apart, and putting things together. He can use his mouth to taste, to kiss, to blow out a candle. He can change his shape, lifting his arms over his head and bending into a squat position.

This year, your child will be particularly busy developing both his gross and fine motor movements. Gross motor movement is the development of the large muscles he uses for sitting, crawling, standing, walking, and climbing. Small motor movement involves the hands and fingers, eye-hand coordination, and his ability to grasp things, build block towers, place puzzle pieces, hold and roll a ball, put shapes in same-size holes, and so on.

Your child's self-image

Somewhere between 13 and 15 months, your child may become absorbed when looking in a mirror, intrigued by a familiar image, though not yet aware that the face smiling back is himself. If something is different about this image that he doesn't recognize—the result of a new haircut, perhaps—he may touch the mirror rather than himself to examine it better. At about 18 months old, he begins to understand that the familiar image is, in fact, himself, and, when confronted with a change in appearance, will touch his own face rather than the mirror image to examine the difference.

He can also look at photographs and is able to identify himself in the pictures. He may even turn to you in amazed delight, while pointing to a picture and say, "Me!" or his name. In fact, this is about the time he will probably start using pronouns, such as *me, I,* and *mine,* to refer to himself. Midway through this year, he may be able to say his own name, and he'll do it with great pride. He certainly responds to his name and loves games that ask, "Where is ———?" All of these milestones indicate that he can now view himself as a separate person that others see from the outside, as well as the person he feels from the inside. At this time you might notice that he begins to have definite opinions about what he wants to wear and how he wants to look, since his internal sense of self is based so much on how he appears to himself.

His awareness of his body extends to recognizing parts of himself. Before he can talk, he will understand the names for different body parts and delight in showing you where they are when you name them. Then he'll switch roles and have a good time showing you where your nose, eyes, mouth, hair, hands, feet, toes, tummy, belly button, knees, and arms are. When he begins to talk, he'll have fun taking over the naming himself.

As he begins to associate sensations and control of movement with different parts of his body, he will feel pride and enthusiasm over having a body. You may find that he will begin shedding clothes as quickly as you dress him simply because it feels wonderful to run around naked and feel sensations that clothing doesn't allow. He also wants to be noticed and admired for the wonderful physical being he is.

Your toddler may grow fascinated by the things his body produces. This may include an interest in the mucus from his nose when he has a cold, his urine and feces, the spit from his mouth, and the passing of gas. He has no idea about social conventions and wonders why you might react with disdain if he offers you anything that his body has produced. Because of his belief that his body parts and products are important parts of himself, he will react strongly to parting with any of it. Thus, he may object to haircuts, nail clipping, and even tossing away a soiled diaper. During this year, you'll need to be especially sensitive to your child's fears about parting with any essential part of himself. You may want to clip his nails when he's asleep. (He won't notice this change in himself if he doesn't see it occurring.) You may want to join him in getting a haircut, first showing him how you sit for a trim and then encouraging him to do the same. Most toddlers are well used to seeing dirty diapers tossed away and won't mind as long as you don't make a show of emptying feces into a toilet and flushing them away.

When appearances change

Changes in his appearance especially trouble your toddler. For example, seeing a scratch on his nose or a spotty rash in the mirror may cause him to worry whether he is still himself. A trickle of blood from a scratch can be a big surprise and a terrifying experience. He may never have seen anything like it before, especially coming from his own body. Your reactions to any mishaps that cause bumps and bruises or blood loss will either soothe him or upset him further. A calm approach and a reassuring "when we get cuts a little blood comes out" helps your child take these events more in stride. If your toddler has a nosebleed or other injury that results in a fair amount of blood, try not to let him see it. If he has a very visible facial rash, don't make a big deal out of pointing it out to him. When he catches sight of himself in a mirror, simply say, "you have spots now but they will go away."

While appearances are of the utmost importance to your one-year-old, he will not be aware of anything about his appearance that differs from other children, so something like a birthmark or being of a different race than a playmate will not concern him. Changes in himself matter most.

Changes in the physical look of those closest to him can also prove upsetting, however. If dad shaves off his beard, your child may not recognize him at first. If any important person in his life suddenly shows up with a drastic change in hairstyle and color, the change may unnerve him. You can lessen the impact of a change on your child by allowing him to watch the transformation; let him watch you put on makeup or get a haircut, for example. Seeing you or others in a costume, particularly a face mask, will be frightening. This is why it's best to limit Halloween to simple costumes and not take your toddler trick or treating until he is older. (Fears are discussed in more detail in Chapter 7.) Seeing people whose appearance differs greatly because of cultural differences—such as seeing a person of another race—will fascinate your toddler and he's likely to stare or even cry until he is content that the new look falls into a category that he already understands.

Awareness of genitalia

In his second year, your child will become more aware of his genitals and the differences between anal and genital sensations. He will probably discover that touching his genitals feels good. Be assured that at this age, such touching is not sexual per se in either girls or boys, but rather springs from the same impulse that causes your toddler to want to touch, taste, and handle anything.

Along with his discovery of his body parts, he may also begin noticing gender differences between himself and other children, beginning the process of categorizing people as males and females. By around 18 months, most children have established their gender identity and clearly recognize themselves as either a boy or a girl, though it's not until around age three or four that they realize that their gender identity doesn't change over time. Because children are especially interested in things that are different from their own bodies, a boy may become interested in his mother's body while a girl becomes intrigued by her father's. Toddlers with siblings, and those in day care who are likely to see other children naked or during diaper changes, may become interested in looking at and touching one another's genitals. It's a good idea to tell your child that he can't touch everyone, but do so in a calm, reassuring way.

Gender differences in physical, emotional, and cognitive development

Physically, boys and girls do differ somewhat in physical development. Boys tend to be taller and heavier than girls and have greater muscular strength, although the differences are usually slight from 12 to 24 months. Boys and girls are about equal in their physical activity level, however, and for toddlers of both genders, movement is their primary focus.

The differences in how they move are subtle. Boys are more likely to demonstrate gross motor behaviors, such as kicking their legs and waving their arms, while girls tend to concentrate earlier on fine motor skills, such as holding a cup. Girls often are more physically coordinated and more expressive in vocalizing and smiling. Researchers have found that girls' early social skills garner more verbal attention from their parents, further widening the distance between girls' and boys' verbal skills. In other words, because girls talk earlier and more often, parents engage them more in conversation, enhancing their lead. Parents of boys need to provide opportunities for their sons to enjoy the give-and-take of talk to help them develop their verbal skills. Likewise, parents of girls need to provide opportunities for their daughters to participate in full-body movement, giving them the chance to increase their gross motor skills.

At the toddler stage, when your children are just beginning to form ideas about what it means to be a boy or a girl, it's crucial that they are not restricted to activities that are gender specific. Both boys and girls should be able to play with dolls and tea sets, and trucks and balls, so that all aspects of their personalities and their physical abilities can thrive. Both boys and girls need to be allowed a full range of emotions, too, so that it's fine for boys to cry and not expected that girls will always be cooperative.

Your child's gender role is strongly influenced by his environment and the behaviors he imitates. Be careful to encourage your child's self-esteem and pride in a gender-neutral way.

Compliment boys and girls for showing nurturing behavior. Being kind to another child, a stuffed toy, or a pet deserves praise.

Give both sons and daughters ample opportunities to meet physical challenges. Pay special attention not to inhibit a girl's physical activity with too many reminders to "be careful."

Give your toddler opportunities to see boys and girls and men and women in a variety of quiet and active roles. Choose books that feature gentle heroes and able heroines.

Acknowledge feelings without regard to gender. After all, it's confusing for a boy who's sad or hurt to hear, "Big boys don't cry!" when he knows they do.

Avoid gender stereotypes in your praise. Don't use words such as "sweet" or "pretty" to describe a girl and "strong" or "smart" to describe a boy. Both sons and daughters are sweet and pretty and smart and strong and enjoy hearing a wide range of positive statements about them.

How it feels to be me

It's so much fun to be me. I love to run and climb and splash and laugh because I can. Every day I'm amazed at what my body can do and produce all by itself. Finding out what I can do makes me want to try new things and also do what I know over and over again. I love to look at myself, too. It's exciting to learn that I have a nose, ears, fingers, and toes like everybody else, yet not exactly like everybody else.

CONFLICT
What separateness means to your toddler

Your toddler's mastery of movement usually coincides with a realization that he is a separate person who is able to stray far from you. While this can be an exhilarating and powerful realization, it can also be scary and make him feel vulnerable. You may see this clearly when he wanders away from you, then realizes how far he has gone, and runs back to climb into your lap. He will want to be reassured that you are within easy reach in case he needs you.

Because of this conflict between wanting to explore his new-found independence and not going too far from your comforting presence, at around 18 months you may notice an increasing anxiety over being separated from you even for brief periods. (See Chapter 9 for a further discussion of separation anxiety.) This is a normal phase your child will go through while he tries to sort out the combination of fear and excitement he feels. Besides separation anxiety, he may also become more demanding and tearful when he doesn't get what he wants. Minor bumps may cause unusual distress, and he may become upset when something breaks or disappears.

Setting consistent limits will help him feel more secure as he deals with becoming a separate person. Although he feels powerful, this power can frighten him. He wants to control what he does, but he doesn't yet have judgment.

Little by little, your child will learn to handle the opposing pulls of attachment and exploration in his own way. Having you as a secure base will enable him to make the transition as smoothly as possible.

YOU AND YOUR CHILD
Enhancing your child's self-image

To help your toddler feel pride and comfort in his body and what it can do means being able to accept him just as he is and remembering that everything he experiences is new and wonderful. When your child does something new, such as climbing stairs, praise him for his accomplishment before you tell him he might have gotten hurt. When praising, don't make comparisons with other children. For example, instead of saying, "You run faster than all the other kids," just say, "You can run fast. That's wonderful." This also applies to things he is not able to do as well as others. Praise him for what he can do and encourage him to continue trying.

Similarly, when it comes to your child's appearance, don't criticize or label him. For example, if you are ready to go out and you see that your child's hair needs combing or he has just gotten his face dirty, don't say something like "You're always such a mess." Instead, you might say, "Your hair is a little tangled in the back. Let's brush your hair so you can look your best."

What if your child is different in some way? He may be oversized or have a noticeable birthmark or a disability. In this case, helping your child develop self-esteem and pride in his body is especially important. Focus on what your child does well and encourage him to do everything he can. Be matter-of-fact to others who may inquire. And don't get caught up in others' insensitivity. For example, if your child is tall for his age, others may assume he is older than his actual age, and they may be surprised when he cannot do things that older children are already able to do. They may want to know why he doesn't talk yet or why he still wears diapers. Just tell them how old he is and explain that he's tall for his age. You don't have to say anything more. And you will have preserved your child's self-esteem, as he is likely to know the conversation is about him and will sense your reassuring manner. If you are anxious or upset, he may wonder if he caused it and feel badly about himself.

When your child does something you feel is unacceptable, such as showing you the mucus he has taken from his nose, giggling when he farts, or proudly demonstrating how he can direct his pee, try not to overreact. Such situations will give you an opportunity to talk about how interesting bodies are, how they are alike and different, while teaching the difference between public and private behavior. Above all, try not to embarrass your child for doing what comes naturally.

In addition, you can help your child develop a positive self-image if you remember not to push him into achieving developmental milestones before he is ready. Be assured that he is developing at his own pace. If pushed, he may become unsure and lose confidence.

Encouraging your child's physical development

Because your child's physical body and sense of self are so closely linked, gaining physical skills will go a long way to giving your child a strong sense of his own worth. There are many activities that your child can do alone or with you that will encourage the development of his physical abilities.

Fine motor skills
To improve hand and finger coordination:

♦ Provide tissue paper, wrapping paper, or paper towels that your child can tear, crunch, and fold.

♦ Tie favorite toys with plastic chain links to your child's high chair and stroller. He will be able to knock and toss them away and not lose them. Pulling up the chain to retrieve the toy will also provide a challenge.

♦ Provide a box with compartments, such as a cardboard six-pack soda container. Give your child paper-towel tubes or plastic bottles to put into and take out of the compartments.

♦ Set up a bowl of water or put some water in the tub. Provide plastic cups of different sizes that can be used to pour. Allow him to experiment with different objects to find out if they float or sink. Have him retrieve sunken items. Show him how to squeeze a wet washcloth. Let him try splashing the water with different objects.

♦ Wrap a toy in paper and ask your toddler to unwrap it to find out what is inside. Use different kinds of paper to wrap objects.

♦ Give him containers with lids, such as yogurt containers or shoe-boxes, and encourage him to take off the tops and put them back on.

♦ Invite your child to imitate various motions you make, such as wiggling your fingers, holding circled fingers in front of your eyes, clapping hands, or curling his fingers into small circles.

♦ Introduce him to crayons and other writing tools and encourage scribbling. Likewise, provide finger-paints, clay, and other tactile materials for your child to manipulate.

Choosing toys that aid your child's physical development
In addition to the toys that help your child develop his large muscles, listed in Chapter 1, these playthings will help him develop his smaller muscles:

♦ Nesting cups and shape sorters give toddlers experience matching what they see with how to move their hands to make the toy "work."

♦ Chunky crayons and clay will help your child learn to control his fingers.

♦ A large doll with clothing will give your child the opportunity to try taking off and putting on clothes.

♦ Balls and pull toys will help develop gross and fine motor skills as well as eye-hand coordination.

♦ Hats for your child to try on and take off easily—especially in front of a mirror—will give him practice in self-dressing skills as well as help him to have some control over his appearance.

Normal physical milestones

As your child develops physically, at times, you may be concerned that he is not keeping up with what others his age can do. Development covers a wide range, and it is likely that your child's physical progress is perfectly normal. The following guidelines for when a skill may first be mastered and when it should be mastered can help alert you to any lags. If your child has not reached the milestones in the "should be able to" column by the age given, you may want to consult your child's doctor.

13 months

Should be able to
- move into a sitting position (beginning around 9 months)
- pull up to a standing position
- move from place to place while holding on to furniture or your hand
- clap hands

May be able to
- put an item into a container
- stand unaided
- drink from a cup
- point to a particular object
- scribble with a crayon

14 months

Should be able to
- stand alone
- wave good-bye
- put an object into a container
- bend over and pick up an object

May be able to
- walk well
- imitate dumping an object
- build a tower of two blocks
- run
- walk up steps holding on to your hand or crawling

15 months

Should be able to
- walk well
- drink from a cup
- scribble with a crayon
- point to a particular object when asked

May be able to
- point to a body part when asked
- use a spoon and fork
- pretend to feed a doll

Normal physical milestones, continued

16 months

Should be able to
- imitate activities such as dumping an object from a pail or box

May be able to
- kick a ball

17 months

Should be able to
- build a tower of two blocks

May be able to
- walk up steps holding on to a railing or higher steps
- take off an article of clothing
- build a tower of four cubes
- throw a ball overhand

18 months

Should be able to
- run well
- use a spoon or a fork
- point to a body part when asked without gestures

May be able to
- follow a command of two steps

19 months

Should be able to
- walk and run with ease
- walk up steps with confidence

May be able to
- build a tower of four to six blocks
- wash and dry hands
- name up to six body parts

Normal physical milestones, continued

20 months

Should be able to
- use a spoon and fork
- throw a ball overhand

May be able to
- name and identify one to four pictures
- build a tower of six blocks

21 months

Should be able to
- point to and name one body part
- kick a ball forward
- point to and identify at least two pictures
- take off an article of clothing

May be able to
- put on an article of clothing
- brush teeth when helped

22–23 months

Should be able to
- build a tower of four cubes
- follow a two-step command
- identify and name six body parts

May be able to
- point to and identify four pictures
- wash and dry hands
- jump up

24 months

Should be able to
- take off an article of clothing
- pretend to feed a doll
- build a tower of four to six blocks
- throw a ball overhand
- point to and identify up to four things in a picture

May be able to
- jump
- build a tower of eight blocks
- draw a line

Gross motor skills

To help your child develop his ability to use his arm and leg muscles:

♦ Lay a small book or other object on the floor and invite your toddler to jump over it. Try other actions such as stepping over the item backwards and walking around it.

♦ Have your child climb up on a low, strong box or a stair and give you both of his hands, and then jump to the ground after you say, "Ready, set, go!"

♦ Show your child how to walk and use his arms to imitate different animals.

♦ Set up an obstacle course, such as chairs that you can walk around to give your child practice with changing direction. You might even drape a blanket over the chairs to make a tunnel you can both wiggle through.

♦ Play music so your child can dance to different rhythms.

♦ Place rice in an oatmeal box or plastic container with a lid. Seal the container and give it to your toddler to shake while you sing and dance together.

♦ Take off your shoes and show your toddler how to wiggle his toes. Continue with the head, shoulders, hips, hands, legs, and so on.

♦ Sing the "If You're Happy and You Know It" song and have your child clap and wave hands, touch his nose, tap his feet, and so on.

♦ Demonstrate different movements that you know he can do and invite him to imitate you. For example, you might squat down, run across the room, or roll on the floor.

Developing your child's senses

Your child uses his senses naturally as he explores his world. He touches different surfaces, manipulates objects, smells things, watches what goes on, enjoys tasting, and listens to all the sounds around him. These activities can help make your child more aware of his senses:

Sight. Because your toddler's eyes are not yet able to focus easily on everything in his environment, you can help him take in the many images he sees during the day.

♦ On outings, call attention to something specific in a larger scene, such as a dog playing with another child, someone roller skating, or a child riding a bike in a larger playground scene.

♦ Show your child his reflection in a mirror. Also show him what toys and other objects look like in the mirror.

♦ Invite him to look at objects through a sheer curtain and a colored glass.

♦ As he nears his second birthday, get an unbreakable magnifying glass and show him how it makes objects look larger. Encourage him to examine a number of objects—including himself and you—through the magnifier.

♦ Ask him to point to specific parts of pictures as you read a picture book, finding, for instance, the cow in a barnyard scene.

Sound. Because your toddler is so focused on speech, he is less aware of other sounds in his environment. To help him tune in:

♦ Call attention to a clock ticking, a bird singing, an airplane flying overhead, or a dog barking, and talk about the source of each sound.

♦ Introduce words that describe noises, such as loud or quiet. You might put your hands over your ears to demonstrate loud or your finger to your lips to demonstrate quiet. Encourage your child to use these signs to communicate to you before he's able to say the words "loud" or "quiet."

♦ Teach your child some of the various sounds animals make, such as: a dog barks, a cow moos, a chick peeps, a duck quacks, a lion growls, and an owl hoots. Begin by naming the animal, then make the sound and have your child imitate you.

♦ Expose your child to a variety of music styles.

♦ Whisper.

♦ Allow your child to make his own music by clanging spoons, playing a toy instrument, and banging on a pot.

♦ Give your child things, such as plastic lids, blocks, a spoon, and a bouncy ball, to drop. Encourage him to listen to the sound each object makes.

Smell. Your toddler doesn't yet distinguish most "good" smells from "bad" smells, and will not, for instance, be troubled by the odors in his soiled diaper. He is, however, naturally drawn to sweet smells and will recoil from strong odors such as vinegar. To hone his sense of smell:

♦ You can expose him to a variety of smells by taking a "smell walk" around your home. You can smell a fresh flower, the laundry from the dryer, a piece of fruit, meat that has just been put on a platter, baby lotion, just-baked cookies, strong-smelling cheese, vanilla, spices (but not any he could inhale) tuna salad, lemon juice, and fresh bread.

♦ Outside, while on a walk or shopping, you can search for freshly mown grass, pine needles, fresh herbs, even the smell of the air.

Taste. Taste is a sense a bit more difficult to explore with your toddler, especially if he is a picky eater and is unwilling to try new things. To encourage exploration of tastes:

♦ Start with the foods he does like, take a bite yourself, and use simple words to describe what you taste, such as sweet or salty.

♦ Also experiment with taste textures, such as soft, hard, crunchy, creamy, and juicy.

♦ Regularly encourage your child to try something new. However, don't push him to taste something he doesn't want to try.

Touch. Your toddler naturally uses his fingers to explore every part of his world. You can increase his awareness of the many textures he experiences in these ways:

♦ Guide his hands over many different textures, such as Daddy's unshaven cheeks, a fuzzy sweater, a silky shirt, a fluffy cotton ball, crinkly dried leaves, a tile floor, sandpaper, a furry pet, a wooden box, smooth metal, and so on.

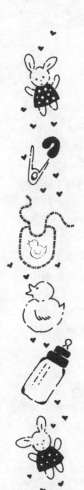

I've got an idea!

Your toddler's thinking skills and learning style

When you catch a glimpse of your child carefully examining a feather, "feeding" her teddy bear, repeatedly practicing jumping off a step, or simply running joyfully across a lawn, you are watching her mind as well as her body at work. Observation, mimicry, repetition, and, most of all, unstructured play are the means by which your toddler experiences the world. Through all her experiences, she develops her brain, makes connections, and solves problems—the cognitive development that proceeds rapidly this year.

DEVELOPMENTAL MILESTONE
Memory and problem solving

By the time your child reached her first birthday, her brain was 90 percent of the size it will be as an adult. During early infancy, your child learned to exercise her inborn reflexes, such as sucking and extending and retracting her arms and legs. By her fourth month, she was busy learning to coordinate eyes with hands, and eyes with ears, batting her hand in the direction of something that interested her and turning her head in response to a sound. By about eight months, she tried to elicit a response from her actions and anticipate the results of those actions. For example, she hit a noise-making toy to produce a sound, and, after repeating this action a number of times, learned to predict the sound even before performing the action of hitting the toy. Between nine and twelve months, she became increasingly curious, which, aided by her new mobility, inspired her to explore.

By age one, your child understands that objects exist even when she can't see them. She can think about objects and events that are not right before her eyes. This development, known as "object permanence," is an aspect of her developing memory and allows her to hold an image of people or things in her head even when she cannot see them.

Throughout this year, all of your toddler's experiences enhance her cognitive development. She will expand her ability to categorize. Already she groups people into those she knows well and trusts and those who are unfamiliar. Meeting an unfamiliar person causes her anxiety as well as heightens her interest. She also has begun to categorize people as male or female, adult or child, and recognizes that she falls into the "child" category. Therefore, she doesn't always feel stranger anxiety around unfamiliar children since she is aware that they share characteristics with her. Her categorizing extends to objects and animals, too, although she may over- or under-categorize. For example, if she is familiar with dogs but few other aninals, she may think that all animals are dogs. Or, she might consider her dog and Grandma's familiar dog as "dogs," but exclude other, unfamiliar dogs from the mental category.

She has a primitive understanding of cause and effect, knowing, for example, that if she tosses a block it will make a particular sound and that its impact can knock over another object. To develop an understanding of cause and effect, she will repeat actions over and over to test if the same action produces the same response each time.

When she plays with a toy, tries to reach something, or curiously opens a cabinet door to see what's inside, your child is developing her problem-solving abilities. Her quest to understand how things work starts with a trial-and-error approach. This is similar to when she learned about cause and effect by experimenting with new and different approaches until one action produced the desired result.

Already, your toddler has all the tools she needs to begin learning about the world around her. Her curiosity, creativity, and persistence show that she's an explorer, a scientist, and an artist who enjoys experimenting, discovering, and creating. Her cognitive abilities will continue to grow, but even at age one, she's remarkably aware and knowledgeable.

How toddlers learn

Your one-year-old is a learning machine, taking in information by observation, testing her ideas through experimentation, and constantly practicing what she is learning. All of her activities, particularly unstructured play, provide lessons from which she can learn.

Unlike older children and adults, who can rely on their years of experience to infer the result of their actions or the properties of an object, your toddler needs to use her senses to explore every aspect of the object she is learning about. In addition to using her hands, she uses her eyes and ears, and she may smell and taste an object, even if it's something, such as a wooden block, that a more experienced person would not consider worthy of such attention.

She'll shake an object to better understand its properties, asking herself, "How heavy is it? Does it make noise? Will it change shape if I squeeze it? Can I take it apart? What's inside? What will happen to it if I drop it? What does it taste like?"

If a familiar item changes, such as a dress that gets torn or a toy car that loses a wheel, she may be alarmed and want to show you the change for you to acknowledge it, too. She will notice changes in her environment, such as a repainted room or a new chair, and will want to examine the change closely. When you talk to her about changes, she's reassured that you're aware of them, too.

Mimicking your actions is a particularly fun way of learning by observation. You pick up the phone and speak into it. She does the same. You say, "uh-oh" when you drop a book and she echoes, "uh-oh." You eat with a fork, and she insists on doing the same. Ironically, much of her quest for independence from you takes the form of trying to copy the things you do.

The next step in your toddler's learning experience is problem solving. Motivated by her innate curiosity, she's driven to discover and figure out things on her own. One day she'll learn that there's a "right" way to put on a sweater. But for now, she's content to find a creative solution on her own, and won't be troubled by the fact that the sweater may be inside out, upside down, and backwards. If her current goal is to figure out how to get her arm into a sleeve, that's all that matters to her. Sometimes, you'll see frustration building as she tries out solutions that don't further her goals. It's good to give her a moment to struggle with finding a new solution rather than jumping in to solve the problem for her. Asking, "Can I help you?" will give her the opportunity to choose you as part of her problem-solving strategy without having to cross the line into tears or to give up.

Another learning tool that is particularly appealing to toddlers is repetition. Repeating an action over and over again helps your child "hardwire" the information and offers proof that the world is predictable. For instance, your toddler may spend a lot of time playing with a plastic drinking straw. She may bend it dozens of times, each time waiting to see if it will spring back to its original shape. Until she's repeated the action often enough, each time getting the same reaction, she's not willing to give up her experiment. Once she's satisfied that the straw has predictable qualities, she can move on to examining something else. If you closely observe her repeating an activity, you might notice that each time she does it she introduces a slight variation. Each of these variations teaches her something new and interesting. If she is confused about what she is doing, the repetition helps her to figure things out.

Her interest in repetition extends to your interactions with her. She'll want you to read the same story again and again. With each reading, she wonders if the same events will take place. She feels a certain excitement as she anticipates what will happen next and is downright relieved when her predictions come true. Toddlers who are as yet unable to discuss their fears also benefit from the repetition of a familiar storybook or video in that any aspect of the story that frightens them or confuses them can, with many retellings, become less scary.

Your toddler observes your routines and is comforted when your actions follow a reliable script, too. For instance, if you always take your backpack with you when you head out the door, your toddler may remind you of it and try to drag it to you, if you're leaving without it. Her own routines help her learn about the way the world works, too, and when she's settled into a bedtime routine, she may become anxious if that routine is altered.

Predictable outcomes have many learning benefits for your toddler. When she knows what will come next, she can feel powerful in that knowledge. Also, being able to count on regular routines frees your child to spend her mental energy on things other than the exhausting process of trying to figure out what might happen next in all situations.

Learning styles

As we've discussed, most toddlers learn by examining and doing. But beyond this method of gathering information, you will begin to see an emerging style of learning that will be unique to your child and will be the way she approaches learning later on.

Educators have determined that most children develop a distinctive learning style that fits within seven broad categories or types of intelligence. No child uses only one style, and as children grow, different styles may be more evident than others.

Linguistic learners absorb information best by reading, writing, telling stories, and playing word games. As toddlers, they love to talk and they listen intently while you speak.

Logical-mathematical learners think in concepts. They learn best by asking questions, figuring things out logically, and experimenting. They gravitate toward science and math. In toddlerhood, they particularly love to solve puzzles and manipulate objects.

Visual-spatial learners think in images and pictures. They learn best by drawing and designing. They excel in art, love to build with interlocking blocks, and enjoy mazes, picture books, and movies. They are wonderfully imaginative, which can manifest itself in extensive daydreaming. In the toddler years, a visual-spatial learner may enjoy building and drawing.

Bodily-kinesthetic learners are physical. Most toddlers can be considered kinesthetic in their drive to move and explore. Kinesthetic learners dance, run, jump, build, touch, and gesture. They love movement and drama, sports and physical games, and learn best with hands-on experiences.

Musical learners are music smart. They sing, whistle, hum, tap their feet and hands in rhythm, and enjoy listening to music. They love to sing and play musical instruments. Other types of learning may seem boring to them.

Interpersonal learners like to bounce ideas off other people, and they tend to be the leaders and organizers of groups. They usually have a lot of friends and enjoy being a part of community events, clubs, group games, and social gatherings. Toddlers with an advanced enjoyment of peers and who show natural curiosity and empathy toward others may be interpersonal learners.

Intrapersonal learners are more introspective. They love time alone to think about things, to make their own choices, and to work on their own projects. They often learn best by setting goals, keeping journals, and having time to daydream. Some people may think of intrapersonal learners as loners. Toddlers who show an ability for solo play early on may become lifelong intrapersonal learners.

Elements of all the learning styles can be found within every person. And these elements usually work together in complex ways. However, by the time your child is in elementary school, you will find that she favors one approach more than others.

Learning curves

There are certain cognitive milestones that can help you determine if your child's cognitive development is proceeding as it should. As with physical development, children develop their mental abilities at varying rates, and just as early walkers may not be star athletes in high school, a child's early cognitive development is not a perfect predictor of academic excellence. But, like physical development, there are predictable stages that can serve as guidelines in evaluating your child's needs.

Around 13 months. Your toddler is an explorer. She studies everything through her senses by picking it up, examining, testing, manipulating, and perhaps putting it in her mouth to taste it and bringing it to her nose to smell it. She begins to understand object permanence by looking in the right place for a ball that has rolled away and is hidden under the couch. Concepts enter her mental vocabulary. In other words, she becomes aware of the meaning of ideas as well as objects. Ideas such as "up" and "down" and "in" and "out" become clear to her. She notices the properties of objects, and may arrange toys in size order or may group toys of one color or type together. She is still, however, in a concrete stage of her thinking, living entirely in the present. Her imagination is not yet developed, and abstract thinking is not yet part of her mental repertoire.

Around 15 months. By this point, your child begins to make connections between ideas and objects. For example, she will see how size and shape affect her play, testing to fit smaller objects inside larger ones, stacking blocks by size, or putting two like objects—such as a train and a track or a doll and a stroller— together to enhance her play. She introduces an element of story-telling sequences into her play when, for example, she scoots her toy boat across the surface of her bathwater and then sinks it. Her interest in picture books becomes heightened as she learns that the illustrations represent real things in her world.

Around 18 months. By now your child has become a scientist, experimenting further with the qualities and possibilities of any object she can grasp. While her earlier relationship with the objects was primarily tactile, now she mixes in ideas. She begins to use toys to act out her ideas, using a doll to represent a baby and a toy truck to represent vehicles she sees on the road, for example. Imagination sets in, too. She may be able to use objects symbolically, pretending, for instance, that a pillow is a doll or a spoon is a truck.

She focuses on the qualities of the objects with which she is playing, testing out, for instance, how sand, water, or wooden blocks fit differently into the same container. She takes great pleasure in imitating your actions, such as dusting off the table after she eats if she has seen you do the same. She may start trying to ask questions, either verbally or by handing an object to you, using her body language to communicate that she wants to know more about what she is examining.

While her concept of time is still vague, the idea of "now" and "then" is taking hold. She can now recall, for example, where she left a toy and that she was playing with it, so that she can continue to play with it after taking time out for a nap or lunch. She begins to understand that when you say "now," as in "Let's have lunch now," something will happen right away. When you say "later," she knows she will have to wait. She's also more aware of her environment, both how she can affect it and any changes that take place within it. For example, when she flips on a wall switch, she knows a light will come on.

Around 21 months. Your child is now able to distinguish some shapes, understanding, for instance, that wheels and balls are circular. She may wonder where things are when they are not in sight, and you may find her hunting for something and then showing delight when she discovers it. This is very different from simply happening upon an object to explore; now her actions are more purposeful and she will ignore the puzzle you've placed in front of her if she is thinking about playing with a ball.

She also understands routines and the connection between events. For instance, when you say, "Let's go out," she may hand you her jacket. She can now appreciate the plot of stories that you read to her more than just enjoying the pictures and the sound of your voice, and she will notice if a picture is upside down. This is a common time for a love of nursery rhymes to develop. She knows her name and can point to basic body parts. Her ability to categorize expands beyond people and things she sees daily to people and things she encounters in the larger world. She also is developing some idea of past and future, and may nod when you ask, "Do you remember what we did at the park yesterday?" and will understand the meaning of the words later and soon to mean "not now."

Around 24 months. By this time, your child is becoming a planner. She will be able to think in images, categorize things, arrange them in different kinds of order, and make judgments. She may be fascinated with broken objects. Her memory has developed considerably. Her sense of time has also developed so that she can now anticipate events. She is able to think of more abstract concepts, such as later and sooner, same and different. Her imagination has also expanded, and she begins to play creatively rather than just imitating what she sees and hears. She can draw simple pictures (though you may not yet be able to identify the objects she draws) and may be able to copy lines and circles. She now becomes a problem solver who can set goals and work on ways to reach them. If she does something wrong, she may be ingenious enough to say someone else did it or at least to say "No" when asked if she misbehaved. She may use the word "I" in reference to herself, can identify people's gender, and begins to recognize gender role differences she observes in society. For example, she may identify certain clothing as girls' clothing while other clothing is considered boys' clothing.

It's important to remember that there is a wide range of normal. It's also critical to remember that, while some aspects of intelligence may be genetically predetermined, what a child does with her potential is not. Manifestations of intelligence are influenced by her physical health, her experiences, and her own learning style. The most crucial factor in whether your child will reach her potential, of course, is you. When your child feels safe and nurtured, is encouraged to experiment without fear of making a mistake, and is given the opportunity to have a variety of experiences, she will grow intellectually to her fullest.

Is there a problem?

While not achieving specific cognitive milestones according to the usual timetable does not indicate that a child is lagging per se, certain behaviors (or lack of them) do signal the need for an evaluation by your child's doctor. Underlying physical problems, such as a hearing loss or a chemical imbalance (hyperactivity, difficulty solving age-appropriate problems), can interfere with a child's cognitive development. The behaviors to watch out for include:

- Taking an unusually long time to complete a task that peers can readily accomplish.
- A lack of coordination between hand and eye movements and/or a stiff or awkward gait.
- Showing only limited interest in new and unfamiliar people and things.
- Difficulty solving problems that are age-appropriate, such as stacking two or three blocks, sorting a few items by shape or color, or finding an object hidden under two or three covers.
- Very limited vocalizations, including few words and phrases.
- Difficulty following simple spoken directions.
- Inability to recognize or point out familiar objects in a picture when asked to do so.
- Regression, including losing skills she once mastered.

When development is slower than average

Certain genetic conditions, including Down syndrome and fragile-X syndrome, which are detected in infancy, can interfere with a child's ability to learn at the same pace as other children. Subtler conditions present at birth or that can develop later may also limit a child's ability to learn. Many of these are correctable and all children can benefit from early intervention to overcome the effects of a genetic condition, chemical imbalance, or physical injury. If your child does not appear to be progressing as she should, have her evaluated by her pediatrician, who may refer you to a specialist to uncover the source of the delay. You can also work to enhance her learning and reduce her frustration in these ways:

Enrich her language environment. Make a special point of talking to her and engaging her in conversation. Read to her.

Demonstrate how to use objects. Show her, for example, ways to open and close a container or stack blocks. Be careful in doing so not to show any frustration of your own if she doesn't respond immediately to your instructions.

Engage her in physical activities. Because she may be content to sit and watch the action, it could be tempting to allow her to spend too much time on the sidelines. Give her the opportunities she needs to stretch and exercise her muscles.

Encourage her to socialize. Make sure she has many chances to interact with other adults and children. If her abilities are not always on par with her peers', arrange playdates with younger children or children her own age who share an interest with her.

Is your child gifted?

Of course she is! Every child has her own special talents, whether they be intellectual, artistic, social, musical, or anything else. If your child is exceptionally alert, curious, quick to learn, and shows evidence of a good memory, she may very well be gifted intellectually. Children with above-average intellect also need special attention. However, this does not need to include formal testing to evaluate her abilities; IQ tests and other assessments at this age tend to be inaccurate. You can help support your child's intellectual development in these ways:

Enrich her language experiences. In everyday conversation, introduce synonyms to expand her vocabulary. Introduce concepts such as opposites; comparisons, such as big, bigger, and biggest; and sequence words, such as first, next, and last. Regularly read aloud to her.

Give her a variety of opportunities. Your child is far too young to be given any kind of formal lessons, but you can introduce her to music, art, and other activities that challenge her and hold her curiosity. For instance, let her examine toy or real musical instruments, and show her how they make their sounds.

Don't push. It's tempting to offer your child many choices, but be careful not to overstimulate her. Like all children, your child needs down time to pursue her own interests at her own pace. Be careful not to get into any habit of asking her to perform for you or others, as this could rob her of her natural joy in doing what she does well and could limit her explorations into other areas of interest.

Recognize her limitations. Though your child may be far ahead of her peers in some areas—like counting, for example—it is likely that there is some area in which she lags behind them. Make sure that she has the opportunity to practice things, such as kicking a ball, that may not be her primary interest, so that she can develop other necessary skills.

Help her learn to socialize within proper norms. While it's important that she has friends who are emotionally and physically on par with her, guard against allowing her to take over the play in every situation. Make sure she has friends with whom she can share her interests, perhaps children who are a bit older than she is and to whom she can look for leadership.

Imagination and pretend play

One of the hallmarks of your child's second year is her burgeoning imagination. In play, it begins with her ability to pretend that a toy stands for something real, such as a baby doll standing in for a real baby, and moves into the ability to use one item to represent another. She might, for example, make believe that a chair pillow is a car. She then moves along to mental storytelling, "driving" her pretend car to the store, even making tooting noises to imitate the honking of a horn. Or, if she doesn't have a play telephone when she wants to play with one, she might be perfectly content to speak into a banana.

She'll pretend to clean, cook, or read the newspaper in just the same way you do. As she becomes more involved in make-believe, she will probably want to involve you, too. She might want to feed you and comb your hair, just as you do for her.

In the second half of her second year, your child will begin to combine make-believe actions, showing her deepened understanding of sequence and problem solving in her thinking. For example, she might perform several pretend activities with a doll, such as taking it for a ride, tucking it in for a nap, and reading a book to it. Her developing language skills will enhance her ability to make believe, and, by her second birthday, she may invite you in to her pretend play.

Make-believe activities that your child initiates are fun for her. But since she can't always distinguish between real and fantasy, she may be upset and frightened when you pretend, or when she sees television shows or videos that include images and actions that don't represent the real world as she knows it.

Your toddler's sense of humor

As your child's intellectual abilities develop, so does her sense of humor. By observing what she finds amusing, you may gain a major insight into how your child learns and thinks.

During infancy, your child laughed in response to a pleasant physical sensation or a broad smile from you. This year, what she finds funny is usually related to the ability to remember objects that are out of sight and the ability to anticipate something. When the expected result turns out differently, your child is surprised and so laughs.

At some point, your one-year-old will make her first joke. It might be in response to a question game that you've played before.

For example, if you ask her, "Where is your ear?" she might smile slyly and point to her nose even though she's pointed to her ear on all previous occasions. Or the humor might be physical. For instance, she might place a sock on her head and move into your line of vision wearing the sock and a big grin. Now that she knows that a sock goes on a foot, the juxtaposition startles and delights her and she wants you to join in the fun. If you then put a mitten on her foot, she might laugh out loud.

As your toddler learns to speak, she may begin to enjoy silly word games. She may take a word that sounds funny to her and repeat it over and over in a singsong rhyme. She might also invent nonsense words to rhyme with other words.

As her sense of humor develops, she will also try to attract your attention by joking. If there is something your toddler knows she shouldn't touch, she might reach out for it in your presence with a mischievous little smile on her face. If you respond with a tone that shows you know that she's being silly, she may break into a fit of giggles.

CONFLICT
When skills lag behind ideas
Learning to think about things in new and different ways is exciting for your fast-growing toddler. How wonderful to suddenly have a great idea and think, "What if I did..." or, "I wonder what would happen if I..." and then try it out.

However, your child will often become frustrated when she can think of a new idea, but doesn't have the ability to turn that idea into an action. If she sees something new that she wants to investigate but is unable to reach it, she may become angry. If she watches older children playing on playground equipment and can't imitate them precisely, she may cry or even have a temper tantrum. If she wants to change the position of a chair and isn't strong enough to do so, she may continue trying until she is exhausted and tearful.

As your child grows stronger and more dexterous, her repeated attempts to try new things will usually be successful. Until that time comes, though, she may need you to decide when she needs to be redirected or gently helped to accomplish something. Always give her a chance to figure out something for herself within the bounds of safety. You may be surprised at how clever your little experimenter is. However, if you see her about to collapse with frustration and anger, it's time to step in. Luckily, your one-year-old also has a short attention span, so if you can successfully distract her with something else that's interesting, she may forget what so frustrated her only a few moments before.

How it feels to be me

I am thinking of you, even when I can't see you. This image of you in my head makes me feel closer to you but also makes me aware that you're not really here. Now that I can picture you, I miss you and may get very cranky and nervous thinking about you. I have lots of ideas in my head that I can't share with you completely yet. I may show you something so that you can explain it to me. Or sometimes, I just want you to see what I'm working with and I don't want you to talk to me about it.

Now that I know a lot about how the world works, I am startled when things are different than I've learned. I find some things scary and some things very funny. I like to play games with you to let you know that I understand things. Isn't it funny when you ask me to point to the sky and I point to the ground? I want you to know that I know I'm not supposed to touch the television. So I make a noise so that you can see me get close to the television. I'm smiling when you say, "Don't touch," because I want you to know that I understand.

Creating an environment for learning

Far more important than mastering facts at this stage in your child's development is learning how to learn. In some ways, of course, your child instinctively knows how to learn by testing, experimenting, and handling objects. But your response to her instinctive learning methods teaches her important lessons about how to learn. Your approach affects how she feels about herself as a learner, how much risk taking she's willing to handle, and whether she will appreciate the process of learning as much as the results. To help create a home environment that supports your child's learning:

Support your child's style. If your child likes to take things apart, find objects that she can safely manipulate. If she likes to be on the go most of the time, don't attempt to slow her down for a midday story time.

Celebrate even the "mistakes." When your child turns a cup of water over and soaks herself, a lighthearted response like, "Oh, look what happens when you turn over the cup! The water goes from the cup to you!" rather than, "You've made a mess!" lets your child understand about cause and effect rather than frightening her or sending the message that her curiosity was somehow bad.

Focus on the process, not the result. When your toddler stacks blocks, she's learning about physics, and about her own power to affect the world. If she's about to place a block in such a way that the tower will fall, let her. Don't step in and caution her about the upcoming "failure." Even if she's disappointed that the tower collapses, the learning process would be incomplete if you protected her from it.

SAFETY FIRST
Lead poisoning alert

Exposure to any toxin can hamper your child's ability to learn. Lead, especially, can retard cognitive development and even cause brain damage in large doses. Lead exposure may also cause behavior problems, hearing and attention deficits, and kidney damage.

The greatest exposure to lead can come from chewing objects covered with a lead-based paint, eating flakes of lead paint and plaster from chipping and peeling walls, or inhaling dust that contains lead particles. If you live in an old house, have the paint and plaster checked for lead. Call your local EPA for information on testing services and local laws. Other sources of lead poisoning may be materials containing lead used in a hobby or job, and a nearby industry that uses chemicals containing lead, which might be released into the air, water, or soil (such as a battery plant). A child may be more susceptible to lead poisoning if her diet is high in fat and low in calcium, magnesium, iron, zinc, and copper.

Lead in drinking water can come from the water system or leach in from lead pipes or lead solder in the plumbing. If your house, apartment building, or water main was completed, replaced, or replumbed after 1986 (when laws outlawed the use of lead pipes and solder), you need not worry. Otherwise, it's a good idea to have the water tested from each faucet used for drinking. Collect water when you first turn on a faucet in the morning. You should be able to get the water tested locally, or call the Safe Drinking Water Hotline (800-426-4791) for the closest facility.

If you do find lead in your water, you don't need to replace all of the plumbing. Just make sure that you run the cold water until it is cold to flush out any lead that has accumulated. Make sure you use only cold water for drinking and cooking. If you are concerned about wasting water, save the first water for cleaning and garden uses.

Your pediatrician can determine if your child has been exposed to lead through a finger-stick blood test. If the result shows a high level of lead exposure, consult a specialist for the best treatment. Lead poisoning is most often treated with chelation therapy and iron and calcium supplements which help to remove excess lead from the body. Chelation therapy is a process by which doctors inject medicines that help rid the body of lead. The medication helps bind to the lead in the blood and greatly increases the body's ability to eliminate it.

Symptoms of lead poisoning include:

Headaches	Weight loss
Irritability	Poor attention span
Abdominal pain	Noticeable learning difficulty
Vomiting	Slowed speech development
Anemia	Hyperactivity

Give your child opportunities to search for solutions. Don't rescue your child when she's frustrated in a learning task. To know when to step in, watch carefully to see when her frustration level rises to a point where she can't go any further in trying to solve a problem. A certain amount of frustration is important in the learning process. Intervene only as much as necessary to keep her in search of a solution. Make suggestions, show her a way to do it, or show her the first step, then let her take over again. Be available to help with the next step if necessary. If it's something she is determined to figure out, be patient in allowing her to try again and again. You may be surprised at how persistent she is.

Accept that learning can be messy. Since your toddler uses all of her senses to learn, she will most likely make a mess and get dirty in the process. Squishing mud through her fingers is delightful, and she'll learn a lot about mud as well as about what her fingers can do in the process. You can limit the mess a bit by having drop cloths available before your child undertakes a finger-painting project, but accept the fact that messes happen. Realize, too, that helping you clean up is a learning experience.

Set as few limits on exploration as possible. Interrupt only when your child is doing something that is truly beyond her capability, unsafe, or against the rules of the household. Explain why an activity is not allowed, and then try to distract her with another activity.

Don't focus on performance. Your child is delighted to show off what she's learned. It's important, however, that you don't ask her to display her talents repeatedly for the benefit of an audience.

If your child...	Do say	Don't say
seems to be struggling with how to use a toy	"You're working hard at figuring it out."	"That's too hard for you. Let me show you how it works."
shows you an object, such as a new toy stuffed giraffe	"You have a giraffe. Would you like to talk about the giraffe?"	"I'll tell you all about this giraffe," then not give your child an opportunity to talk about it too.
uses an object to stand for another object, such as using a banana for a toy telephone	"Hello. Is the phone for me?"	"That's not a phone. It's a banana. Bananas are just for eating."

Developing your child's cognitive skills

The play your child engages in every day and the routines that are part of her regular schedule teach your toddler what she needs to know. These activities can enhance the natural learning that will take place this year:

Ask and answer questions. Talk with your child, even if she can't yet keep up her end of the conversation. Encourage her verbalizations. Answer her questions, which may be in the form of words or body gestures.

Encourage experimentation. Though your child is naturally experimenting with all manner of items, you can broaden her understanding by joining in her explorations. For example, if she's splashing in the tub, offer her plastic bowls and measuring cups to play with. When she discovers a dandelion puff on the lawn, show her what happens when you blow on it and let her try to blow on it, too.

Expose your child to a wealth of experiences. Vary the daily routines enough to provide something new every so often. Take her out of the familiar environment of home and visit playgrounds, neighborhood stores, the post office, a beach, and so on.

Involve your toddler in household routines. Find tasks that she can do. For example, when doing the laundry, you might give her one towel to fold, or when it's time to feed the dog, let her scoop out a cup of dog food and pour it into the dog's bowl.

Introduce her to various tools. In addition to learning how to use a spoon and fork to eat, your child will enjoy using a variety of art and kitchen tools, such as crayons, or spoons to help you stir a salad. Show her how the doorbell works and how to flip a wall lightswitch.

Encourage fantasy play and make-believe. She may be interested in make-believe as early as her first birthday, or not until she
is nearly two. By observing how she plays, you will notice when she
is pretending. Join in if she initiates a pretend-play session with
you. Ask questions and make comments, but don't try to direct the
play. Also provide materials that encourage pretend play, such as
play dishes, pots and pans, toy vehicles, puppets, and so on.

Look for toys that will spark her imagination. Examples
include dolls, stuffed animals or action figures with clothes that are
easy to put on and remove, a doll bed, a toy stroller, a small comb
and brush, plastic food (that's not too small), a doll bottle, small
empty boxes, plastic cups, play dishes, a toy telephone, hand puppets, a truck that can be filled and emptied, a play purse, hats, and
other dress-up clothes.

Provide materials that encourage problem solving.
Examples of these include puzzles, nesting containers, blocks that
stack, and shape boards. You can also model problem solving by
sharing with your child how you solve a problem. For example, if a
door squeaks, you might tell her verbally what you plan to do to try
to stop the squeak, such as putting a few drops of oil on the hinge.
She can then go with you to get the oil, watch you put it on the
hinge, and help you test the door to see if the oil worked.

Should I try to teach my child?

You may be eager to encourage the learning process that your toddler is engaged in by providing rewards for things like letter or
color recognition and counting. While it's true that some toddlers
are able to learn certain facts and can recall letters, colors, and
numbers, few children grasp the real meaning of these symbols
before the age of three or four.

Even if your child appears interested in flash cards or magnetic
letters or numbers, rote learning is not a natural process for toddlers

and it cannot provide the deep learning that comes from experience and experimentation. Children who are rushed into learning academic skills often develop anxiety about making mistakes and certainly lose some of the joy that natural learning gives them.

To prepare your toddler for the academic learning that will come in a few years, you can find toddler-appropriate activities that facilitate the understanding of reading and math that will come later:

Provide a language-rich environment. Read to your child. Talk to her and encourage her to share her ideas. Point out signs, such as stop signs, to demonstrate the use of color and letter symbols in the world. Playfully introduce rhymes and songs so that your child attunes herself to the sounds and meanings of words.

Teach math concepts naturally. Talk about how you set one plate for each person. When you share a treat, point out, "One for me and one for you." During a game of naming body parts, note that she has one head and one nose and two eyes and two ears. Talk about shapes, perhaps noting that "the ball is a circle and the pizza is a circle." Keep it simple.

Point out colors. As she approaches her second birthday, your child may begin to understand colors and will enjoy going on a hunt with you as you point out all the red things you can find and then all the blue things. Don't expect her to be able to name or differentiate many colors just yet.

Television and toddlers

In limited amounts, television and video watching can be entertaining parts of your toddler's learning experience. Shows designed especially for young children can help broaden their vocabularies and give them another way to learn about the world.

Because this learning is passive, however, it's no substitute for the active learning that best suits a toddler's learning style.

Inappropriate images seen on programs intended for older kids and adults can frighten young children. Even some children's programs, such as cartoons that contain acts of violence, should be avoided since studies show that regular viewing leads to increased aggression. Watching too much TV (the recommended limit for one-year-olds is half an hour a day) before the preschool age has also been associated with poor behavior and delays in reading readiness when children start school.

Videos for toddlers

When choosing tapes, look for engaging music and stories that will encourage an interest in books and the world itself. Many children's libraries rent tapes, and your local librarian may have suggestions for your child's viewing. These are good examples of toddler-appropriate videos:

♦ *Are You My Mother?* (Sony Wonder; 30 minutes) Three stories by children's author P. D. Eastman make a fun extension of reading time.

♦ *Babymugs!* (MVP Home Entertainment; 30 minutes) This entertaining tape features babies laughing, gurgling, and mugging for the camera.

♦ *Happy Birthday, Moon and Other Stories* (Children's Circle; 30 minutes) This tape includes five short stories, which can be viewed individually.

♦ *Sesame Street Sleepytime Songs & Stories* (Sony Wonder; 30 minutes) This calming tape is great for down times.

♦ *Where's Spot?* (Walt Disney Home Video; 30 minutes) Four stories are included, featuring the daily life and activities of a puppy named Spot.

Encouraging solo play

A toddler cannot play on her own for any extended period (half-hour to an hour). But being able to entertain herself for brief periods (10 to 20 minutes) contributes to her sense of independence and helps enhance her creativity. Self-reliance is a learned skill. You can help your child gain some experience in organizing her own time in a number of ways:

Practice moving farther and farther from her as she plays with a toy. Keep yourself within her view, though, so that when she looks up to find you she doesn't have to interrupt her play by getting up and searching for you anxiously.

Make sure she has easy access to toys that she can play with on her own without too much frustration. Toys that respond with a noise or movement after a simple touch from her can hold her attention for minutes at a time. Other good solo toys include blocks, books with easy-to-turn pages, boxes, pots and pans, dolls, and action figures.

Consider placing a child-safe mirror or other reflective surface at your child's eye level. Watching herself play is great fun for your toddler.

Praise your child as she spends time in solo play. Don't be afraid of "breaking the spell" by interrupting her. Your encouragement lets her know that what she's doing is valued.

Gaining experience with everyday activities

Besides playing, exploring, and investigating, your child also wants to learn to do many of the daily activities you do for her now. You may find that she wants to take the comb away from you to try to comb her own hair. She may refuse to let you dress her because she wants to do it herself. She may not want to open her mouth to eat unless she gets to hold the spoon. All of these activities are things she needs to learn to do, and her determination to accomplish these tasks lets you know that she's ready to begin these self-care activities. To help her along and to satisfy your own need for accomplishing tasks without too much fuss:

Make eating easier. Before meals, place a plastic cloth under her chair so that messes will be easier to clean up. Then provide foods that are simple to pick up with the fingers or that stick to the spoon or fork. For example, mashed potatoes are a better food than soup when learning to use a spoon.

Be patient. Give your child the time she needs to accomplish each task. If you find that things are taking too long, you can join her in her self-care tasks. For instance, you can feed her one spoonful of food and let her feed herself the next.

Look for shortcuts. Choose the right tools to help your toddler accomplish what she wants to—chunky crayons, a wide-toothed comb, and clothing that is easy to put on and take off, for instance.

Offer assistance. For early attempts, guide her if necessary and tell her what steps she should follow. When dressing her, for example, give her step-by-step instructions: "Put your arm in the sleeve first. Now try the other arm."

Praise attempts. A remark such as "You tried to put on your own mitten" lets your child know that you've noticed.

My many moods

Your toddler's feelings and emotions

Your toddler's emotional range includes the same happiness and sadness, trust and fearfulness, love and anger, joy and sorrow that you experience. Unlike an older child or an adult, however, your one-year-old is not yet attuned to his feelings and thus may be surprised and overwhelmed by them. Nor does he have the ability to control his reactions to his moods and he will act out his feelings rather than process them intellectually. Though he cannot control his feelings and his reactions to them, his reactions are no longer purely reflexive and he is more aware of his feelings—and the feelings of others.

Your child's emotional responses to the world are influenced by his temperament, his language skills, and his experiences. Understanding the reasons behind your toddler's emotional expressions will help you better understand his feelings and help him—and you—deal with them. Your primary job this year is to provide the emotional safe haven your child needs while giving him the tools to regulate his responses to his emotions.

DEVELOPMENTAL MILESTONE
Awareness of feelings

Your child's understanding of emotional relationships began in his first year. In his first few months, he was able to recognize which people belonged to his family and which didn't belong. He saw himself, of course, as the center of the family orbit. This awareness formed the foundation for his emotional development.

As a one-year-old, your child learns how his emotions are intertwined with his experiences. He can show you his love with hugs, smiles, and gentle pats. He may demonstrate anger by hitting or biting as well as crying. He may be alternately trusting and cooperative, or frustrated and resistant.

At around eighteen months, he begins to think about his feelings rather than simply experiencing them. He may be able to use words to name his emotions. During play, he may start to demonstrate the emotions he experiences, comforting a "sad" teddy bear, for example. In this way, he illustrates his new understanding that he can have an impact on the emotions of others.

Most likely, he began this year readily displaying his affection for you. As his surge toward independence and his newfound mobility take over, he may become less demonstrative, even pushing away from your attempts to cuddle. On some days, he will simply be too busy to land in your lap for a hug or kiss. The next day, however, once he's mastered the skill that had kept him occupied, he may take the lead in showing you his love. This pull-and-push is a sign that your child is developing normally.

Temperament and emotional development

Your child's temperament greatly influences his emotions and the intensity with which he experiences them. Temperamentally challenging toddlers are more likely to have emotional swings, going from joyous to tempestuous and back again quickly throughout the day. Slow-to-warm-up kids and those with easy temperaments are more level in their show of emotions, though they experience the same range of feelings. You'll find their changes of mood easier to understand because the shift from one to another will take place at a slower pace. Active kids will rarely slow down enough for long cuddle times, nor will they stay in a bad mood for long, since getting up and moving are their primary goals.

Within his own temperament type, your toddler may be more or less sensitive, distractible, intense, persistent, adaptable, regular, or moody than children of other temperaments. If your child is more sensitive, he may tend to cry easily if startled by noise or activity, if someone is upset with him, or if he is put in a new situation. If he adjusts easily to new situations, he's likely to be happier and more easily comforted when he's upset. If he's shy or slow to warm up, he may exhibit anxiety if pushed into a situation he's not ready for. A persistent and intense child may be more easily frustrated and fretful and so seem quick to exhibit anger or to whine. If your toddler's intensity level is low, you may have trouble discerning what emotions he is feeling.

Of course, no matter what your child's temperament is, there will be times when he will be happy or sad, anxious or calm, angry or fearful like everyone else. Regardless of temperament, certain experiences evoke certain responses in most kids. Enjoying the safety and security that you and the company of other people who love and care for him provides will result in a general feeling of calm and happiness. Separation brings on sadness and fear. Having his desires thwarted will make him angry and frustrated. Simply being hungry or tired or in a new environment can trigger emotional outbursts.

The importance of trust

This year, your child's intellectual development allows him to know that there's a larger world than what he experiences at home with you. He has begun to understand that he is separate from you. While these are exciting developments and he's naturally driven to explore as much as he can, the knowledge that he exists as a separate person in a large and unknown world can create a great deal of anxiety. Your presence gives him the courage to continue growing into his separateness. You are the stable base from which he can confidently explore. When you comfort him, encourage his explorations, provide a safe harbor to return to when he needs reassurance, he absorbs the confidence you have in him and feels it himself. If, however, he didn't receive the loving care he needs, his anxiety would overwhelm him and he would be far less likely to venture out as he needs to.

Your child's trust in you and the care you provide allows him to give full play to his emotional repertoire. He can get angry, knowing he won't be rejected. He can be sad and frightened because he knows you are there to comfort him. He can be joyous or simply contented because of the constant of your love for him.

Your child's trust can be undermined if you or others on whom he depends for care are unresponsive to his needs, push him into situations that he is not prepared for emotionally, or are erratic in responding to him. If, for instance, he hurts himself and is not comforted, if he's frightened by an activity and is prodded to take part anyway, or if words don't match their emotional content, he will be confused by his feelings and will not readily learn what they mean or how to respond to them himself.

Stages of emotional development

From birth to the age of two, your child moves through distinct stages of development in which his emotions mature alongside his cognitive skills. The challenges of each stage must be met and mastered before a child can move on to the next stage.

Stage 1: Birth to Three Months. During this phase, your newborn had to learn to calm himself, control his body movements, and focus his attention on a world that may have seemed overwhelmingly noisy and full of lights, smells, textures, tastes, and temperatures. In order to concentrate on the most interesting sensations, he had to learn to organize them in his mind, learning, for instance, to tune out the sound of traffic outside his window, while concentrating on the sound of your voice. Visually, he learned to separate your face from the background. As his needs for food, warmth, and touch were met, he began to experience the world as predictable and trustworthy—crucial to his feelings of safety.

Stage 2: Three to Four Months. After your child was able to focus on you rather than succumb to distractions, he began to enjoy spending time with you, especially when you talked to him, imitated his sounds, and smiled when he smiled. These interactions gave him a sense of humanity, which forms the basis of later feelings of compassion, love, and empathy. Without this intense bond, he would have a hard time seeing beyond himself, feeling a sense of community with other people, and taking pleasure in relationships with others. Along with the calm and happiness that he felt, his emotions widened to include anger, pleasure, and contentment.

Stage 3: Four to Ten Months. A major change occurred between four and ten months, when your baby began to see that his actions caused others to react. For example, when you responded happily to his smile, or you picked him up when he stretched out his arms, he began to understand the two-way nature of emotions. Your understanding of his communication signals became a great source of satisfaction for him. If you had been unresponsive, he would have become apathetic and become much less interested in communicating. Cut off from a sense of community, he would have had a harder time learning that other people are separate from him and are able to do and feel different things.

Stage 4: 10 to 18 Months. By his first birthday, your child began to communicate with you more in order to learn more about his world and what he can do within it. For example, when he looks at you questioningly, you may ask "Where?" or "What?" to which he might respond by pointing to something or leading you somewhere, making sounds and pointing all the way. When you figure out what he wants, he responds with nods, smiles, and perhaps a laugh. If you ignore him, he'll become frustrated and angry, or passive. At this stage, he learns to read your emotions and body language. Just from watching your posture, gestures, and expressions, he can learn a great deal about feelings. He may have already discovered that when you look sad, you won't be as willing to respond immediately to his requests. He may be well on his way to knowing which of his behaviors make you angry and which win your approval. If a child at this stage feels pushed away or rejected in any way, he may disassociate from his emotions or may begin responding aggressively to you and others.

Stage 5: 18 to 30 Months. In the last half of his second year, your child begins acquiring language that will allow him to name not only things and people, but feelings, too. His emotional experiences with things, people, and sensations help make meaningful the connections between images and words. He can learn to describe his feelings rather than simply acting them out by saying "Don't want to"; "I like"; or "I sad." During this stage, particularly, it's essential that your words reflect your feelings. For example, when praising him, he needs to hear the enthusiasm in your voice as well as your words. Likewise, when correcting him, the tone of your voice along with your words needs to register disapproval.

During this period, your child will increase his understanding of the emotions of others and may laugh or cry simply because another child is laughing or crying. This is not mimicking behavior but is an actual reflection of your child's ability to empathize and sympathize with others.

The emotionally-healthy toddler

Toddlers' behavior is ruled by emotions. One-year-olds are often overwhelmed by their feelings and may lose control occasionally. Showing extreme feelings on occasion is not a sign of any problem. Rather, the lack of visible emotion, a very narrow range of emotional responses, or a sudden change in a child's overall emotional demeanor *can* signal an emotional difficulty that you should discuss with your child's doctor. Signs of emotional well-being for one-year-olds include:

♦ A strong attachment to parents and other primary caregivers.

♦ A selective attachment to others, which is shown by a wariness to people he does not know.

♦ Being able to accept brief separations from you.

♦ An interest in the world around him.

♦ A demonstration of a full range of emotions—negative as well as positive—such as anger, love, stubbornness, fear, sadness, and anxiety.

♦ Appropriate responses, such as anger at being thwarted or happiness when being given positive attention.

How your child shows love

Around his first birthday, your toddler began finding many ways to express his love for you. Since he is naturally drawn to your face, he may already be giving you affectionate pats on the cheek. He may progress to pats on the shoulder and then to hugs. However he shows you his affection, he is demonstrating that you are someone he trusts to be there for his needs, to comfort him, and to understand him. And now that he is mobile enough to reach out, touch, and hug your whenever he gets the urge, he may surprise you now and then with seemingly out-of-the-blue demonstrations of his affections.

The ability to share and express love is important to your child's emotional development. Recent studies have shown that loving interactions are crucial to cognitive development. Loving interactions have an affect on how the brain grows and the number of connections formed between nerve cells.

Through this second year of his life, you may find that his demonstrations of love vary in intensity and in frequency. When he experiences a sudden surge in motor development, he'll be much more interested in exploring his environment than taking time out for a hug. When he finds something new, however, you may notice that he always runs back to you to share it with you in some way.

If he feels overwhelmed by his newfound skills, you may find him suddenly clinging to you and wanting to cuddle on your lap. And, by around 18 months, you may discover that he shows his affection by screaming every time you leave the room because he is afraid of being separated from you. (You will find more on separation anxiety in Chapters 7 and 9.) Even though such loud displays may be disconcerting, they are still an indication of how important you are to your child.

As your child nears his second birthday, he may be able to express his love for you in words by saying, "Love you." At this point, emotional outbursts may lessen somewhat, or be accompanied by tearful explanations of why he is upset.

Besides showing you how much he loves you, your child will shower others with affection. Siblings, caregivers, and even inanimate objects such as a stuffed animal may be regular recipients of kisses, hugs, or pats. However, you will probably notice that each object of affection is treated a little differently. While a baby-sitter may get an affectionate pat and a kiss on the cheek, older siblings may get a fierce hug.

It's common for toddlers to be more attached to one parent than the other at times. A tone of voice or manner may be more appealing or reassuring to your child at different times. It's important not to feel resentful if your child switches his affection to his other parent for the time being. This may change again in a short time.

If your child appears to show affection less openly or warmly than other toddlers, it may be a matter of temperament. Some children don't respond as readily to touch, nor do they express their feelings strongly. If you come from an expressive family, such behavior may be hard for you to understand. But don't assume that he doesn't love you. What's important is for you to observe and be sensitive to how your child does show and want affection. If he doesn't want to hug, you may both enjoy pats instead. Tell your child frequently how much he means to you.

A toddler's feeling of pride and self-worth

Throughout this year, your child is working on mastering several important skills—learning to walk and to talk, figuring out how to feed himself, investigating the things and people around him, and discovering who he is as a separate person from you. He has a lot to be proud of. Your recognition of his accomplishments means a lot to him. When you praise him, he probably beams with pleasure and may strut about like a peacock. He continually seeks not only your approval, but your attention, and when he's doing something that interests him, he'll be anxious to make sure that you take note.

Being corrected as well as earning praise is, of course, part of being a toddler. When you necessarily correct his behavior, be sure to focus on the misbehavior itself and not on your child, saying, for example, "It's not nice to hit," instead of "You're a bad boy." Also, because he can understand far more than he can say himself, be careful what you say about your child when he's within earshot. It's far better for your child to overhear you say something complimentary than to hear how he's been driving you crazy.

Security objects

Besides showing a growing attachment to family members and other loved ones, your toddler may also become strongly attached to a love object such as a blanket or a stuffed animal this year. The attachment may become so intense that your child does not want to part with the object even for a moment.

Security objects, often called "transitional objects" in the parlance of child psychologists, can be important props in helping your child deal with anxiety and serve as substitutes for you when you are not in sight. Carrying the familiar feel and odor of the object from one situation into another helps your child feel more in control. A well-hugged "lovey" can soothe him when he feels tired or upset, and help make a new situation seem less scary.

Attachment to an object usually occurs at around 15 months, when your toddler develops the ability to think symbolically. The object then becomes a stand-in for you and for all that is comforting. The choice of an object is strictly up to your child. You will probably find that you have little say in what he focuses on. It may be something he has cuddled with since birth or it could be something completely new. A blanket is a common choice because it is smooth and soft, like skin and hair. Stroking a blanket reminds your child of your gentle touch. Hugging his lovey while sucking his thumb also reminds him of the pleasant feelings of early feedings.

If your child does adopt an object, remember to treat it with great care and make sure it's available when your child needs it. You may find that you have trouble getting it away from him for washing because he doesn't want you to change the comforting way it smells. If it is a stuffed animal, you may be able to give it a quick sponge bath. With a blanket, you could cut it in two pieces and wash one piece at a time.

Not all children form an attachment to an object, so don't worry if your child doesn't have one. This choice means that your child is able to think of a reassuring image of you without the help of an outside reminder.

Angry feelings

Your toddler's anger can be disconcerting, both in its intensity and its suddenness. It's natural, of course, that your child will feel anger sometimes—when he isn't allowed to do what he wants, for example, or is interrupted while doing something he thinks is fun. You can often limit your toddler's anger and frustration by simply offering alternative activities. If, for instance, he's upset when you tell him to stop playing with the VCR, you might focus his attention on something else that will be equally appealing to him rather than risking his wrath. In fact, knowing how to offer a diversion is probably your best tool in staving off too many angry outbursts.

Sometimes, of course, distraction won't work or your child's anger may be the result of something other than having his desires thwarted. Your response to his anger now will greatly affect how he experiences and expresses anger as he grows. It's vital that he be permitted to feel angry. After all, since anger is a normal emotion, it can't be stopped. How your toddler expresses his anger and learns to channel it, however, can benefit from your guidance. Your first response should be to simply acknowledge it, saying something like, "I know you're angry." If you know the source of the anger, let him know, "It's upsetting that you can't play with the VCR." Then address any misbehavior that accompanies the anger, such as saying, "But you can't hit me." Either ignoring his feelings or his inappropriate behavior is not a good option. (For more on dealing with tantrums, see Chapter 8.)

Jealousy

It's amazing to witness a toddler act like a jilted lover, but jealousy— and its inherent feelings of helplessness, anger, and loss—is common among toddlers. Jealousy is usually centered on loss or a fear of loss. Such fear can be especially intense in the case of a new sibling. The new baby, who is much more helpless than the toddler, will receive a lot of attention from parents and other family members. And just at the time when your child is dealing with his feelings of separating from you, the necessity of having to share you with a baby can be stressful and upsetting. If the new baby or a pet finds comfort on your lap, your toddler may react by trying to squeeze himself between you and the intruder. The best way to handle your tot's bout of jealousy is to include him, whenever possible, in the action, making room on your lap or sharing in the hug. At these moments, it's necessary to reassure him that you love him. But, it's also important to let him know that you love others as well, and that there's plenty of affection to share with the rest of the family. Also make time to spend alone with your toddler and reassure him that he has not been displaced in your affection. (More on helping your toddler welcome a new baby into the family can be found in Chapter 9.)

If your spouse or someone else hugs you, your child may try the squeeze-in maneuver or may physically attack, pushing your admirer away. Toddlers who have developed a relationship with a love object may show their first furious sense of possessiveness when another child attempts to hold or hug their prized blanket or stuffed animal. Though you'll want to start to introduce your child to the concept of sharing some of his possessions soon, now is a bit too early. It's best, then, to support your child's claim on his love object and intervene to retrieve it if another child snatches it from him.

Feelings of shame
Your child begins this year with absolutely no sense of shame. He's delighted with all aspects of himself and is startled and confused when you correct him. As his sense of self develops and he learns what others expect of him, he may, by the end of this year, react with self-consciousness and embarrassment when he is criticized. His expanding awareness that his behavior may not have met with your expectations can even lead to a sense of shame. Unlike guilt, which is an internal feeling of remorse, shame is a reaction to external forces. In other words, your disapproval can make your

child feel ashamed even though he isn't yet able to intuitively know the difference between good and bad behaviors.

Depending on your child's temperament, he may physically sag or even cry when you correct him. Or, he may quickly move on to another activity to distract you from the behavior that earned your negative attention in the first place. It's important to realize that he's not being deliberately defiant; he simply is looking for ways to restore his place in your good graces.

Although shame is an unpleasant feeling, it is an extension of learning social behavior. For shame to serve your child rather than harm him, however, your corrections must be focused on his behavior and not on his worthiness as a person. Saying something like "It's wrong to hit the cat" alerts your child to what is and is not acceptable behavior, while a statement such as "You're bad for hitting the cat" serves more to undermine your child's sense of self than to teach acceptable behavior.

Children can also feel ashamed when they become objects of jokes. Because toddlers can do things they consider serious but that adults find funny, it's often tempting to laugh at them when their actions backfire. For instance, if your toddler reaches for a bag of pretzels and causes the pretzels to rain on top of him, the scene might appear as funny as any kind of slapstick. But to your toddler, your laughing at his mistake can be confusing. Though his sense of humor is developing rapidly this year, he's still not mature enough to laugh at his own foibles. He may cry and become sullen at being laughed at. Depending on his temperament, however, a particularly resilient child may repeat the action to see if it's still funny the second time around.

By the end of the year, your toddler will begin to make the distinction between being laughed at and laughed with. In the meantime, remain sensitive to the possibility that his feelings can be hurt easily.

How it feels to be me

I feel good when you comfort me, and I feel bad when you correct me. Most of the time, I have no idea what gives me my feelings. All I know for sure is that my feelings seem to come from what's happening outside of me. I don't feel in control of my feelings and that's scary.

If I can explore where I want, I am happy. If you stop me, I am sad and angry. If you go away from me, I'm scared. When you return, I cry to let you know how I felt.

It's frustrating to me to have moods that I can't tell you about. Because I can't always tell you how I feel in words, I use my whole body to express myself. Sometimes, I'm so full of feelings that I have to let them out in ways that scare me—like kicking and screaming. I need you to understand that I don't mean to upset you. I need you to help me name my feelings and show me how I'm supposed to express them.

CONFLICT
When emotions overwhelm your toddler

This year, he becomes aware of the full range of his feelings and may become overwhelmed by anger, frustration, fear, and even joy at times.

Without the cognitive ability to recognize his own emotions or the language skills to express what he feels, your toddler will often act out how he feels as his way of processing the feelings. For example, he may suddenly have a burst of activity when he feels excited and happy. He may become whiny and fussy because he has mixed feelings about being independent or simply because he's tired or hungry. If he doesn't want you to interfere with what he is doing, he may rebel and turn every interaction with you into a power struggle. If he is angry, frustrated, or feels powerless in a situation, he may respond by pushing, hitting, or biting as a form of emotional expression and self-defense. If he is fearful or anxious, he may cry from a need to release these powerful emotions. If he has been separated from you for a time, he may save this release until he sees you. For this reason, he may burst into tears as soon as he sees you when you return after a brief separation. Once he feels safe again, he is able to let you know how distressed he had been.

YOU AND YOUR CHILD
The interplay of your emotions

Your own response to your child's expression of feelings has an enormous impact on how your child learns to regulate his emotions. Your calm reaction to all of his emotions goes a long way to assuring your child that you're on his side, that you understand what he's feeling, and that you are there to help him.

Like your child, however, you are subject to your own emotions, and, as the parent of a toddler, you no doubt sometimes feel exasperated, angry, and impatient as well as joyful and contented. You cannot always control what you feel, but unlike your toddler, you can regulate your reaction to your feelings. It's important that you try to be emotionally honest with your child, letting him know, for instance, when his actions truly upset you as well as when he thoroughly delights you. For example, you should tell him that his running away from you scares you, which sometimes makes you angry.

How can you handle your own feelings in ways that serve your child and your relationship with him? The trick is expressing those feelings in ways that support, rather than undermine, your child's self-esteem. This requires that you allow yourself to own your feelings, and that you allow your child to own his. It's important to be able to admit to yourself that you may not always feel as positively toward your child as you may want to, or that your child's rebuff to your hug or kiss might be hurtful to you. Most important, it requires that you don't rely on your child's moods and behavior to define your own.

When you are angry at your child, clarify for yourself if your anger has to do with a specific behavior on his part or with other issues that limit your patience. If your anger is the result of his behavior alone, tell him why you're angry, saying in a stern voice, for instance, "I'm very angry that you ran off when I told you not to." If your anger is really the result of other pressures you're feeling, it's important to separate your feelings from your child. Find another adult to talk with about your feelings so that you don't use your child as a way of releasing steam.

If you're hurt when your child pushes you away, especially when he rejects your affection, it can be difficult not to feel hurt momentarily. But if you find that you're compelled to reject him, too, "to show him what it feels like," you're relying too much on his approval to meet your own emotional needs. Your rebuff will in no way teach him empathy for you, but will confuse and frighten him. It's far better to realize that your child's role is not to prop up your emotional well-being. That's a role for you alone that can be enhanced only by another adult.

Because your toddler wants nothing more than to please you, it's imperative that you don't exaggerate your own emotional response to his actions. You needn't always let him know, for example, that when he plays with his blocks quietly it makes you happy, and that when he reaches for a stick on the sidewalk it frightens you. By maintaining some emotional neutrality, you will give him the freedom he needs to explore. Otherwise, he may learn to always look to you for approval before interacting with his environment, and he either will become too timid or will feel compelled to disregard your feelings.

This year, as he learns to become attuned to emotions—yours as well as his own—he needs reassurance, positive attention, and encouragement. When he displays his emotions, reassure him that what he feels is all right, even when you need to curtail his responses to his emotions. This will go a long way toward teaching him that feelings, both pleasant and unpleasant, are a natural part of everyone's life.

HELPING YOUR CHILD GROW
Supporting your child's emotional growth

Because your child is at an age when he learns by imitation, the emotional model you present is crucial to the healthy development of his emotions. He will notice how you show affection to him, his siblings, your spouse, and other members of your family. He will see how you express and deal with sadness, anger, and frustration. As he observes, he will also imitate. You may notice how he translates what he sees into action when he plays with a doll or approaches another child or adult.

In addition to modeling honest emotion and appropriate responses to feelings, there are a number of things you can do to help your child develop in emotionally healthy ways.

Allow your child to own his emotions. All emotions, including anger and frustration, are normal. Don't short-circuit your child's emotional range by attempting to minimize or dismiss emotions that are on the negative side of the scale. For instance, don't say, "Don't be sad," when your child has every reason to be sad. Instead, acknowledge his feelings in words as well as with a reassuring hug, saying, "I know you're sad."

By conveying the notion that a feeling is not nice, he may begin to feel guilty about experiencing a normal emotion such as anger. If you try to coax him out of a glum, sad mood without acknowledging that it's okay to sometimes feel sad, you will send a message that some emotions are not all right to feel. If you try to contradict a feeling, such as telling him he isn't hurt and is okay after he falls, you encourage him to distrust his feelings. He trusts you to help him identify and label what he feels, and if you give him mixed messages, he will have a hard time recognizing his emotions. By respecting and acknowledging your child's feelings, you will set the stage for him to be able to talk to you about emotions when he has the language skills to describe what he experiences.

Help your child understand what might cause his feelings. Your attention to his experiences reassures your toddler. When possible, let your child know that you are aware of the source of his feelings. If, for instance, your child reacts strongly to the end of playtime in the park, note that you know how it upsets him: "I know you hate to leave the park." Such a statement also gives your child a frame of reference for his feelings, helping him better understand the source of his sudden rage. Be careful, however, not to offer explanations when your child is upset for a reason you don't know. In such cases, as you help your child calm down, see if he can help you understand the cause of his upset, perhaps asking, "Can you show me what made you cry?"

Don't define emotions by gender. It's important to guard against treating a son or a daughter differently when it comes to expressing emotions. Some parents may unconsciously stifle their son's emotions, especially when he cries, because they expect him to "act like a big boy." Although girls and boys may naturally express feelings a little differently, the ability to express emotions is often culturally influenced. Parents may interact verbally and give more comfort to girls without even realizing it. Boys, too, need to be encouraged to express themselves emotionally.

Teach the language of feelings. As your child's language skills increase, help him find words to communicate his feelings. By doing so, you guide him in learning ways to express feelings without acting them out in aggressive behavior, such as pushing, hitting, and biting. When he does begin to verbally express emotions, be receptive to what he says so he knows his feelings are respected.

If you don't readily understand what he is saying, try repeating back what you think you hear. Also pay attention to the gestures and other movements that accompany his words.

Teaching empathy

Your toddler's second year is a time of extreme self-centeredness. His attention is naturally focused on all he can do as he gains skills, particularly walking and talking. He believes that the world revolves around him and that everything he wants should be his, especially now that he can achieve so much on his own. Although he is beginning to understand that other people are separate from him, it's not too early to begin teaching him that these people also have their own feelings that can differ from his feelings. The development of empathy also extends to his understanding that he can affect others' feelings, for instance, causing another child's sadness when he swipes away a toy.

The best way to teach empathy is by showing empathy yourself. You can give your child a hand in understanding how to read body language, cueing him in, for example, that another child's tears signify sadness, or a frown indicates displeasure. Your own matching of words to your facial expression gives your child insight into reading others' emotions, while using words to describe the feelings of others strengthens his understanding.

Because your one-year-old is beginning to understand that symbols can stand for real things, you can also teach lessons in empathy with a doll, showing your child how to handle it gently, how to soothe it, and how to respond to its pretend cry. It will be many years before he is fully able to consider another person's feelings before his own, but taking any opportunity to tell and show him how other people feel will set the stage for this development.

Helping your toddler deal with frustration

It is common for your child to feel frustrated as a result of his own limitations and the limits you place on him; this may often lead to sadness or anger. When dealing with your child's frustration, you walk a fine line. On the one hand, you want to make sure he is safe from danger and not experiencing failure frequently. On the other hand, you want him to be challenged to learn more, which, at this age, comes from experience; this includes testing out ideas, some of which won't work. To limit unnecessary frustration while allowing your child to experience some discomfort, the best approach is to watch your child carefully to ascertain when and if you need to interfere. If he is struggling with something, such as how to use a toy, but hasn't yet reached the point of failure, it's probably best to let him continue. You can stand back or offer a few words of encouragement. When he finally does succeed, the accomplishment will mean much more to him for having worked through the process himself. However, if his frustration is building and he is not moving any closer toward his goal, step in. You might ask first if he'd like your help. You can offer a few suggestions for reaching his goal if he seems interested. If he has taken on something that is clearly beyond his expertise, your best bet is to distract him from the task. You might get him involved in a physical activity to relieve stress, such as dancing to music. You could try getting him involved in an activity that doesn't require abilities he hasn't yet mastered, such as playing with water in the sink, using finger paints, or banging a pot with a wooden spoon. You could also change the scene, such as taking a walk together outside.

Your observations will help you learn what triggers frustration in your child. Then you can look for ways to prevent meltdowns. For example, by making sure he has a snack or a nap, you can head off upsets that often accompany fatigue and hunger. In addition, by childproofing your home, you minimize the limits on your toddler, thereby keeping his frustration to a level he can handle.

Introducing patience

Your toddler lives in the present. Past and future are vague concepts that he doesn't understand. "In a few minutes," "soon," and "almost" are not really concepts he understands, particularly at the start of his second year. Everything your one-year-old wants he wants right now, including things he can imagine that he would like. Since your one-year-old, unlike an older child, will not look forward to events such as a trip to the playground later in the day, his requirements for patience are centered on the present and usually involve a need for your attention right now. Waiting for you to attend to his needs will try his patience.

Other than modeling patience yourself, there is little you can teach your child about developing patience this year. Your job now is to prevent his impatience for your attention from leading to misbehavior. Since this is also a stage of concrete thinking and physical activity, the best way to limit your child's need for patience is to provide an activity that will fill up the time that he is required to wait. For instance, instead of telling him that you can play with him in five minutes, give him an activity he can do until you're ready for him. For example, give him a pot and wooden spoon to play with while you fix dinner.

Here are some additional tips for limiting your child's need to wait or for making waiting more pleasant:

♦ Be prepared with books, toys, tapes, and snacks to pass the time if you are going somewhere that involves waiting.

♦ Cut necessary waiting time as much as possible by leaving it until the last minute. For example, if dinner won't be ready right away, don't put your child in his high chair until just before you put the food on the table.

♦ Don't promise what you can't deliver. If you tell your child that something will happen if he waits, be sure to follow through.

♦ Give your child and yourself enough time to make transitions from one activity to another. Always needing to hurry your child along to the next thing will give him a model of impatience that won't serve either of you well.

Emotional intelligence

Through your help in learning about emotions, your child will have a much greater chance of success in dealing with people in any situation, in making decisions, and in understanding himself throughout his life. This self-awareness is what many people today are calling "emotional intelligence." Coined by Yale psychologist Peter Salovey and John Mayer from the University of New Hampshire, emotional intelligence is now used to describe the qualities of being able to understand and regulate one's own emotions and to have empathy for others' feelings. These qualities constitute what people once thought of as "character." Daniel Goleman, a Harvard psychology Ph.D., believes that intelligence, or brainpower, counts for much less than a person's emotional power in accounting for his or her success.

What frightens me

Your toddler's fears

A few months ago, your baby experienced the world mostly from the safety of your arms, seeing things from your eye level, feeling enclosed and protected. Now that she's mobile, her entire perspective has changed. That, in addition to the cognitive skills she's gaining this year, gives her a new relationship with the world. And it can be scary.

The dog that seemed small to her from your arms is enormous face-to-face. Now that she can wander away from you, she's caught by a sudden realization that you're not right there. Getting into things that earn her a quick "No!" from you is an altogether new and frightening experience. Being aware of her surroundings and developing an understanding of cause and effect make her wonder a number of things: What happens to the water when it goes down the drain? If I can hide from you, can you hide from me? If I'm so angry that I kick and scream, does your anger mean that you're out of control, too?

Your child might be frightened by things like a parent's haircut and resulting change in appearance, or vacuum cleaners, faucets, kittens, and even wind. Your respect for your child's fears, and your patience, will help her deal with them over time. Her experiences as she continues to grow will also help her make judgments about which fears she can safely abandon and those which serve to protect her.

DEVELOPMENTAL MILESTONE
Understanding danger

Fear is a necessary component of survival. Parents teach their toddlers to be afraid of things that are hot, sharp, or in other ways dangerous. You scold your child for running toward the street and she becomes frightened—more because of your tone than the cars, as she doesn't yet understand how traffic is a danger. Your warnings help your child associate danger and fear.

Her push for independence often conflicts with her safety. In her second year, your toddler experiences her first real sense of independence. Her increased mobility will naturally bring her into contact with things and situations that can upset or harm her. She may touch something hot and burn herself. She may reach for a vase and accidentally overturn it. A walk up the stairs can result in a fall.

Her increased cognitive abilities allow her to understand and evaluate her circumstances now. Memory plays a large part. As she recalls burning herself, having a vase land on her, or falling down a stair, she may determine that she doesn't want to repeat such an event and might, for a time, avoid the things that led to any upset. She may overcategorize, becoming fearful of anything that even reminds her of an upset. For example, if your child was scratched by a cat, she may develop a fear of all cats. Fears that result from natural explorations, such as seeing a dog when walking in the park, are more likely to be short-lived since her compulsion to explore will overwhelm her sense of caution. But those fears that are built on singular experiences—being knocked down by a dog in the park, for instance—can take longer to pass.

Your toddler's ability to categorize people into those she knows and trusts and those who are new and different to her may lead her to become frightened of strangers and of people outside her everyday circle, including grandparents and others whom you assume she knows and loves. Stranger anxiety resurfaces and peaks around 18 months. Linked to this fear of strangers is the fear of anything that differs from your child's preconceived ideas of how the world should work and how it should look. Changes in her environment and in the appearance of people she is close to can be disconcerting.

Toddlers are also suggestible; their developing sense of empathy can make them adopt a fearful stance even when they are not sure what it is that is frightening. For example, if another child is afraid of something, such as an escalator, your toddler may have the same reaction even though she was not initially afraid. Your fears can also rub off on your toddler as she learns to mimic the moods of those closest to her. She figures that if you're afraid of something, then she should be, too.

Fears may also come from your child's increasing awareness that she has little power over her life, even as she is first experiencing the power of independence and craving control. Without being able to master her environment or tell you what she needs, she can easily feel helpless, unsafe, and vulnerable, which increases feelings of anxiety and fear.

Common fears of toddlers

Infants are born with two instinctive fears: the fear of falling and the fear of unexpected and sudden occurrences, such as loud noises. During infancy and early toddlerhood, fear of strangers takes precedence. By the second half of this year, your child may be afraid of sudden loud noises whose source she cannot understand, such as thunder or sirens; strange animals, especially dogs; and doctors, who have, in the past, given her shots. Some common toddler fears include:

♦ The sight and sound of the toilet flushing

♦ The dark

♦ Lightning

♦ Noisy appliances, especially the vacuum cleaner

♦ Outside noises, especially sirens and thunder

♦ Going to sleep

♦ Baths, especially the drain

♦ Playground equipment

♦ Masks and unusual facial features

♦ Changes in her own appearance, including haircuts and marks made by cuts and bruises

Temperament and fears

As with other emotions, your child's temperament determines to some degree how fearful she is and how she deals with her fears.

Some children are more anxious and fearful than others. Sensitive children can easily become overstimulated, which may lead to a fearful response. On the other hand, outgoing, active children may seem nearly fearless as they plunge headlong into new experiences with a seeming disregard for their own well-being.

Handling your fearless toddler
Instead of hiding behind your legs when she encounters a stranger, your toddler may greet each new person with welcoming excitement. Instead of wanting to crawl into your arms when she sees a big, strange dog, she may be more inclined to reach out to it. Instead of approaching a street curb or a swimming pool cautiously, she may not look before she leaps, regardless of the consequences. Though active toddlers are apparently fearless, their daredevil ways can terrify their parents.

As a parent of a fearless child, you will need to be extra vigilant in order to stop her headlong rush into potential danger. You'll need to be explicit in defining rules and patient in reminding her of the rules. For instance, if she often approaches strange dogs with aplomb, be particularly watchful for dogs outside. From a distance, point out the dog and say something like, "Let's look at the dog before we get close to it." Then, show her how you ask the dog's owner if you can pet it. Tell your child what you're doing: "We have to ask if the dog is friendly." Show your child how to let the dog sniff her hand first, and then how to pet the dog in a way that won't alarm the animal, gently guiding her hand over its head.

When fears become phobias
Fear is a normal response to a new and frightening situation. In general, your child's fear will pass when the object she fears no longer manifests itself. For instance, your toddler may be terrified of the vacuum as it's pushed around the carpet, making noises and sucking up things in its path. But when the vacuum is standing quietly in the corner, she is not afraid of it.

Unlike fleeting fears about which your child can be reassured, phobias interfere with a child's daily life. In fact, a phobia can be so overwhelming that even thinking about the thing she's afraid of causes your child anxiety. A phobia develops from a fear, but lasts longer and can be even more intense than the initial fear. A scary event, such as being knocked down by a dog, may lead to anxiety even when a dog isn't present. A toddler who has developed a phobia of dogs may become fearful when seeing any real dog or even a picture of a dog. Her growing imagination can conjure up fear, as simply the thought of a dog may make her fearful of entering into a situation in which she might encounter a dog. She may no longer want to go to the park because a dog might be there, and she might cry at the sight of a formerly beloved stuffed puppy. Another common fear that can become a phobia is fear of water. The fear can be so intense that a child will become extremely upset at the sight of running water and will refuse to take a bath. Unlike an adult, who can understand and reason that it's silly to be afraid of water, a toddler has no such perspective to draw on and a growing imagination to fuel her fears.

If a phobia persists for more than a few weeks or if it interferes too much with your child's normal interactions, you should discuss the problem with her pediatrician. Desensitizing your child to the object of her fear will take a great deal of patience. Each step has to be gradual, so that she can become truly comfortable with one stage of acceptance before having to meet the challenges of the next step. For example, you can help a child who is phobic about dogs not to panic when seeing a picture of a dog. Repeated exposures to the pictures from the comfort of your lap can prepare her for the stage of playing with a toy stuffed puppy—perhaps also from your lap. Weeks later she might be ready to move on to seeing a real puppy while you hold her. If she isn't prodded to move along too quickly, losing the ground she has gained, she will, most likely, give up her phobia.

How fears inhibit exploration

Along with your toddler's new bravado and effort to show her independence comes an uneasy realization that the world is big and she is small. Her lack of experience compounds her worries, making her fearful of things that would not scare an older child or adult.

Though your toddler wants to sample all that life has to offer, her new awareness that there are some legitimate things to fear may interfere with her explorations. Her need to put distance between you is offset by her need to have you close at hand. Her need to touch anything within reach has most likely resulted in at least a few hurts that she fears repeating.

The one reassuring constant to your child—ready to take on the world in spite of its scariness—is you. Your encouragement for her to continue to explore allows your child to approach the world with a certain trust. Your reassurances following a frightening event help her confine her fears to the present. Once you have cuddled with her and helped her over her fear, she is able to put it behind her.

Because your toddler may be scared of things that you don't consider frightening, it's important that you be aware of her responses to situations. The same alertness is needed when your child has a sudden fearful reaction to something that didn't trouble her in the past. If, for example, she resists getting into the bathtub one day, it would be easy to mistake her kicking and crying as simple defiance or annoyance that a prior activity had to be interrupted. Taking a moment to listen to her and observe her—a tensed-up body, an inability to be calmed by your words—you may find that her reaction is one of fear, not simply an unwillingness to cooperate. Try to uncover the reason for this new fear so that you might help her overcome it. If she has become afraid of the bathtub, try changing the bath routine, introducing bubbles or water toys or changing bath time. If nothing works, you may simply have to avoid the source of fear for awhile, switching to sponge baths, for instance, in the above example.

Toddlers and Halloween

Parents can get a big kick out of seeing their tots dressed up as princesses, pirates, and pumpkins, and many toddlers really enjoy their new looks. Some, however, will be alarmed by any costuming that alters their appearance too much. Masks are usually uncomfortable and few toddlers will put up with wearing one.

However, seeing their siblings and other bigger kids and adults dressed in scary outfits, complete with masks and face paint, can terrify a one-year-old as can house decorations that depict witches and other characters with unpleasant faces.

If it's possible to steer clear of creepy Halloween displays, do so. If trick-or-treaters come to your door, keep your toddler occupied until you can be sure that their outfits and behavior won't be frightening. Don't prod your child to join in the activities if she shows any hesitation.

YOU AND YOUR CHILD
How your behavior influences your child's fears

Just as your child looks to you for a model of how to express her emotions, she looks to you to know what is and what is not safe, what is worthy of her fears and what is not. Though certain fears can develop seemingly out of the blue, some are based on your responses.

When you respect your child's fears, you don't compound them. Acknowledging her fears with words, simply saying something like "I know you're frightened," gives your child the comfort she needs to begin to sort out her feelings. When you avoid pushing her into situations before she's ready for them, you give her time to reevaluate her fears and to desensitize herself on her own schedule. When you show understanding and support, rather than embarrassment or impatience, if your child is afraid, you give your child the tools she needs to build her trust in the world and lessen her fears over time.

Talking too much about safety, in general, can result in your child being very fearful. No toddler needs constant reminders that the world is a dangerous place. You can also encourage fears inadvertently by being too sympathetic. Keep your responses simple and matter-of-fact. When, for example, your child displays a fear of a dog, hold her and reassure her, acknowledging her feelings. "You're afraid of the dog. I'll hold you so we can watch it together." Adding, "Yes, dogs are scary" and whisking your child away from a situation that is not inherently dangerous will only confirm and deepen her fears. Too much positive attention to fears may also lead your child to feign fears as a way of getting your undivided attention.

You may feel powerless when you find your child terrified, crying, and trembling. It may also seem like you have failed because you couldn't anticipate or protect her from something that is scary. But confronting a fear now and again is the only way your child will eventually learn to cope with and accept the unpredictable nature of life.

If you display a panicked reaction to an event, your child will determine that she, too, should be afraid. Sometimes, of course, developing a bit of fear on her part is a useful thing. If, for instance, she runs off and your fear rises as you search for her, you're likely to show some panic mixed with relief at finding her. When she bursts into fearful sobs at your reaction, she does internalize your feeling that running off can be a scary thing. But an overdisplay of fear can be harmful. If you panic each time she goes just a few yards away from you, she will either learn to ignore your warnings or will take them too much to heart, becoming frightened of the natural explorations she needs to make. If you are afraid of dogs or bees, for example, and you act terrified in their presence or make a show of keeping your child safe from these things, she will adopt your fears unnecessarily. She will be doubly afraid when she feels that you are not in a position to protect her.

When, on the other hand, you model good coping skills, your child will continue to feel safe. She will watch you for clues on how to handle frightening events and will be reassured when she observes you responding with calm and control. When a truly frightening event such as a fire or accident does occur, a response such as "That was really scary, but we're safe now" will do a lot to help your toddler put the scary event behind her.

How it feels to be me

One minute, I am not afraid of anything. That's because I can see you and be near you when I need to be. Then something happens that I don't expect, and I get scared. Anything that seems out of place can frighten me. If I hurt myself, hear a loud noise, turn around and find that you're not there, or get a scary idea in my head from something I saw on TV, I need you to hold me and keep me safe.

Because I need to move around so much, I get myself into situations that aren't what I expected. I climb high, then I can't get down. I run off, and when you don't follow me closely, it scares me. When you hold me and tell me that I am safe, that's how I feel. When you let me take my time deciding whether or not to feel afraid, you make me feel powerful and strong again.

HELPING YOUR CHILD GROW
Helping your toddler handle fears
As toddlers grow and mature, they often outgrow the fears they have experienced and expressed. However, don't assume this will happen without some help from you. It's important now for you to help your child deal with fears so that they won't last throughout childhood. Here are some ways you might help your child overcome a fear:

Offer a demonstration. At age one, your child's limited experience with the world can make certain objects or events seem frightening. If your child is afraid of something because it is unfamiliar, ask, "Would you like me to show it to you?" For instance, if your child is afraid of the vacuum cleaner because she is scared it might scoop her up or because of the loud noise it makes, you might show her that objects as big as a toy, a block, or a shoe can't be vacuumed up. You may want to hold her while your spouse or a friend turns on the machine so she can watch the demonstration from a safe distance. Only do so with her permission, however, since forcing her to confront the source of her fear is likely to increase it.

Read about it. Reading books, besides being a great activity in itself, can help desensitize your child to a source of fear. For example, if your child is afraid of fire engines, you might find a picture book about firefighters and fire engines.

Let your child take some action. Fears are often based on feeling out of control. Showing your child that she can turn a vacuum cleaner on and off with a switch may help her understand that the dreaded machine can be controlled by her. A prop, such as a toy version of a vacuum that she can push around, can also be a handy way to help alleviate her fear of it.

Be sure to give your child stress-free times. Slowing down your child's schedule, giving her lots of lap time when she needs it, and engaging in quiet activities such as taking strolls or listening to quiet music can reduce your child's overall anxiety. If she's regularly on the go and confronted with new and exciting things, on the other hand, the overload itself can make her fearful.

Help others to interact with your child. Older siblings may need reminders that some of their activities are too scary to do around their younger sisters and brothers. Overly friendly adults can overwhelm and terrify a one-year-old with unwanted hugs and kisses. Ask others, even grandparents, to resist coming on too strongly and to give your toddler time to accept their presence before having to show or accept any affection. Explain that your child's reaction shouldn't be taken personally and is typical of children her age.

Avoid the source of a fear for a while. If your child develops a sudden fear, simply avoid exposing her to its source for a week or two. If she's afraid of dogs, visit playgrounds with no-dog policies. If a video frightened her, shelve it for a few weeks.

Don't compare your child to others. Some toddlers are more outgoing and adventurous than others. If you've enrolled your toddler in a parent-child swim class and she's the only one who seems unwilling to join you in the pool, be content to sit on the sidelines with her if that's what she wants. Perhaps by the second class, she'll be more inclined to get her feet wet. Eventually, she will join the others in the water, as long as she's neither prematurely pushed or overly comforted. Never tease or embarrass her for her fears or compare her with other children. As in all things, she needs to be allowed her unique feelings.

Accept that you can't protect your child from all her fears. Some things that frighten your toddler can't be avoided. If your child screams when you approach the doctor's office for a checkup, acknowledge her fear and reassure her that you will remain with her, but be matter-of-fact about being there. Bring a favorite toy or other object along to distract her and make her feel less scared and more comfortable. Explain to the doctor if your child prefers that you be the one to place her on the scale or hold her during the checkup.

Handling bedtime fears

Even if your child has previously fallen asleep with no problems, between the ages of one and two she may begin to resist going to bed, become scared of the dark, and even be fearful of falling asleep. Such fears often come from a reluctance to be separated from the security of parents, toys, and activity and enter darkness, quiet, and solitude. They are also a sign that your child is growing up and becoming smarter.

When she was a baby, she couldn't see anything when the light was turned out. To her, everything was gone and, therefore, there was nothing to worry about. Now, your child understands that even though she can't see something, it still exists. This realization opens up all kinds of possibilities in her growing imagination. Now she can imagine that something she can't see could be dangerous and scary. Though bedtime fears are normal, you can ease them in a number of ways:

Provide a night-light. A soft light can help your child see that the world of her bedroom is unchanged at night. Be sure to use a UL (Underwriter's Laboratory) approved low-wattage compact fluorescent light and to plug it into an outlet away from the child's bed and any other flammable materials. Also make sure the light doesn't shine directly into your child's face.

Encourage the attachment to a lovey. A soft blanket or stuffed animal that always joins your child in her crib can be comforting to her and make her feel as though she isn't alone as she settles in for sleep.

Establish a bedtime routine that is cozy and soothing. Such a routine might include taking a bath, putting on pajamas, brushing teeth, saying goodnight to toys, reading a bedtime story, and turning on the night-light. Playing soft music and spending a few minutes talking about the day can also comfort her. For some children, saying "Go to sleep now" can trigger fears, so instead you might suggest, "Play with your bed toys now," which gives your child experience in separating from you at night without the added stress of having to fall asleep immediately.

Dreams and nightmares

Sometimes your toddler may be awakened by a dream and be afraid of waking up in a dark or dim room, remembering the all-too-real images from her time asleep. Adults and older kids can recognize that "it's only a dream." Your toddler, however, doesn't have enough experience with dreams or reality and can't readily distinguish between the two. So, when she awakens after a dream—whether it be of wild animals or gentle kittens—she will still feel scared and threatened by the unfamiliarity of the mental image. But before going into her room when she awakens in the middle of the night, you might listen for her crying, calling out in a scared or alarmed manner, or making other distressing sounds first. If she does awaken with a fright, it is very important to comfort her right away. It may not be necessary to turn on the light and pick her up. Simply standing beside her and rubbing her back might be enough. But if she's truly terrified, it's best to hold her as she calms down.

Your toddler is not likely to give you much insight into the nature of her dreams through words, but her body language will tell you if she's merely confused about being awake or if she's had a scary nightmare. Nightmares can occur for many different reasons. Your child may be under stress if there has been any tension in the family or if she has been ill. Stress-induced nightmares can also occur as a result of change, such as moving, getting a new baby-sitter, or going into day care. An overactive and developing imagination can also cause nightmares. When your child awakens from a nightmare, calmly reassure her that you are there to protect her. Keep your demeanor quiet and don't insist that she try to tell you what's troubling her. You'll probably need to stay with her until she's asleep again. In the morning, you can ask if she remembers waking up last night, but don't be surprised if she doesn't. Don't probe and don't remind her that she was scared and crying. That will only serve to worry her in the daytime. Try to uncover the cause of any stress and work to reduce it before bedtime. Occasional nightmares are normal, however, and don't require more than your comfort when they occur.

Toddlers can also experience night terrors, which are different from nightmares. A night terror usually occurs between one and four hours after your child goes to bed and when your child is most deeply asleep, whereas nightmares happen much later during the dream phase of sleep or during a light sleep. When experiencing a night terror, your child may perspire, have a rapid heartbeat, appear scared and confused, and cry out for you while pushing you away. She may sit up, try to climb out of her crib, struggle, walk, scream, and cry. Your child's eyes may be open, yet she is actually still sound asleep. Night terrors generally last from ten to thirty minutes. With nightmares, panic doesn't occur until after your child has awakened. With a night terror, your child is panicking in her sleep.

If your child experiences a night terror, there's not much you can do except to make sure she doesn't fall out of bed or hurt herself as she thrashes around. Don't hug her or try to hold her down, as she will become even more agitated. Also don't try to wake her, as this will cause the terror to last longer. After it's over, you can tuck her back into bed for the rest of the night. Your child will have no memory of the event.

Night terrors can occur when a child is overtired or has been overstimulated with too much activity during the day. Most children outgrow night terrors by the time they are six. Realize that, though witnessing a night terror may be upsetting to you, such an event does not harm your child.

Soothing bedtime books

Your local children's librarian will be able to recommend books that are particularly well suited to bedtime reading. These titles are especially appealing to one-year-olds:

♦ *Goodnight Moon* by Margaret Wise Brown (HarperCollins, 1997). Rhyming text and a ritual of saying goodnight to the moon has made this a favorite book for toddlers since the book was first published in 1947.

♦ *In the Tall, Tall Grass* by Denise Fleming (Holt, 1995). This book shows what happens in the tall grass during the day and at night.

♦ *On Mother's Lap* by Ann Herbert Scott (Clarion, 1992). A little Inuit boy finds out that no matter what he puts on his mother's lap there is always room for him.

♦ *Time for Bed* by Mem Fox and Jane Dyer (Harcourt, 1997). Parents of different baby animals help their offspring get ready for bed.

Why I do what I do

Your toddler's behavior

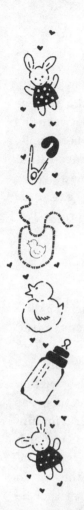

Your toddler's actions will be a mix of kisses and kicks, tenderness and tantrums. This year, he has two overriding forces in his life: to do what he wants and to please you. The conflict that this causes him mirrors some of the conflict that you and he will experience this year.

His mobility may delight you with a made-up dance, but it can also get him into all sorts of mischief now. His increasing vocabulary gives him the power to share an idea with you as well as to give the word *no* a real workout. His memory astounds you as his sure stride into the playground tells you that he recalls being here before and liking it. But he forgets that he's not supposed to touch the knobs on the stove. His exuberant hugs tell you how much he loves you, yet his angry outbursts remind you that he can't always show it.

You will doubtless hit some rough spots during the year as your relationship necessarily includes some conflict between his needs and wants and the needs and wants of you and other people. By setting reasonable limits and helping your child behave within those limits, you increase his sense of security and set the stage for him to develop a habit of cooperation that will make it easier for him to live in the world—and make it easier for the world to live with him.

DEVELOPMENTAL MILESTONE
A will of one's own

This year, your child's mobility and general enthusiasm for life combine with his intellectual and emotional development to lead him to a remarkable discovery: he has ideas that are different from yours. At this stage in his life, those ideas do not concern values—your child has no ability to understand such concepts as good and bad or right and wrong. The ideas that drive his actions this year are all about wants. When an idea strikes him, it is natural for him to pursue it. He sees a button on an appliance. He wants to touch it. Perhaps he remembers that when he touched it before, the TV picture came on. His memory can hold the idea that the button leads to a good outcome—a picture. He cannot remember that he was told not to touch it. That idea, frankly, isn't interesting enough to remember. He may be genuinely startled not only that you don't praise his clever action, but that you correct him for it. As far as he's concerned, pushing the button on the TV is just as praiseworthy as pushing a button on a new toy, something you probably encourage.

Because he's beginning to understand that he is a separate person from you, he's also busy trying to figure out what your ideas are and how that affects your relationship with him. Your toddler may, at times, appear defiant. For instance, he may, immediately after being told not to touch the TV button, look right at you while holding his finger an inch or so away from the button. It looks like he's testing you, and in a way he is. But his purpose is not to misbehave. Rather it's to check out what he's just learned. "Will mommy still say "no" if I try it again?" He may also be showing you proudly that he can resist touching the button, that he remembers your warning (at least in the short term).

Often, your toddler won't mind being distracted from something he wants when you give him something equally interesting to explore. When, for example, instead of saying, "Don't touch," you simply redirect his attention to a more suitable object, he's likely to go along. This way you aren't establishing a habit of confrontation because you've met his need to touch something and you've paid attention to him. If, however, you were to correct him repeatedly without offering an alternative, his need to explore would override anything you have to say.

Punitive responses to your toddler's misbehaviors confuse him and will not result in helping him learn to cooperate. Ignoring inappropriate behavior is not a reasonable course, either, because your child will not learn how to get along with others and how to develop relationships, or how to behave in socially acceptable ways. The middle course of guiding your child toward acceptable behavior while not diminishing his sense of worthiness helps him grow emotionally and socially into a person whose behavior is based on internalized values.

Limiting conflicts with your toddler

As your child's teacher, your job is to guide him to behave in ways that serve him and those around him well. Rather than trying to win battles, you want to avoid them when possible so that his behavior and your relationship are cooperative rather than confrontational. You can do that by limiting the number of rules you impose on him and by providing enough structure for your child to explore safely. These suggestions can help him do what he wants without getting into trouble:

Childproof your child's environment. Careful childproofing will enable you to intervene in your child's actions far less frequently. Removing or hiding dangerous and breakable objects reduces your need to say "No" or "Don't touch." You can't strip your child's environment bare, however, since a sterile, uninteresting home would seriously undermine his development. A toddler-friendly home necessarily includes a great many interesting things. The trick is to make sure that those fascinating things are safe. In every room to which your child has access, keep a basket or shelf of interesting items for him to examine.

Reinforce the idea of "out of bounds" with some hardware. Put gates on stairways so that you need not always have to remind your toddler not to climb. Put window guards on all windows. Put locks on refrigerators, microwaves, and other appliances that tempt your child. To satisfy your child's need to explore and to mimic you, invest in a child-size reproduction of an appliance or build one out of a cardboard box so that he can open doors and look inside to his heart's content.

Make allowances for your child's limitations. Avoid putting him in situations that require more self-control than a toddler can handle. Also anticipate problems by limiting situations in which you know your toddler is likely to misbehave.

You needn't entirely rule out restaurant meals and church services that take an hour or more, but realize that you will probably have to remove your child from the situation now and then to let him run off some steam. If you want your child to be more careful at mealtimes and not spill and scatter food, don't put too much food on his plate. When he finishes one serving, ask him if he wants more. Accept a certain level of mess because your toddler needs to be allowed to explore far more than he needs to be tidy. By limiting his exposure to situations that can cause a meltdown or that might aggravate you, you help make your child's experiences positive, which gives him further practice in cooperating.

Be patient. Realize that your toddler's impulsiveness is not the same as defiant misbehavior. Your child has a limited ability to restrain himself. If you tell him not to touch something, but then don't remove it or distract him, he may be able to resist for only a few seconds before temptation overwhelms him. During this year, you will find his ability to resist will become stronger, but it will take many years before your child will always think before he acts. Don't expect your one-year-old to police himself and to remember that you told him not to do something. For at least another year, expect that you will need to supervise your child constantly, offering frequent reminders about what is and is not allowed. Your model of patience and understanding, as well as your vigilance in keeping him safe, gives your toddler a secure base from which to learn self-control.

Offer lots of positive attention. The more engaged you are with him in general, the more likely that your interactions will evolve in cooperative rather than confrontational ways. When you get down on the floor and show an interest in the discoveries he makes, your child directs his energy toward acceptable behaviors. When you compliment him on being gentle with a pet, thank him for picking up a toy, or congratulate him when he builds a block tower, you reinforce the behaviors you want and let him know that his good actions are rewarded with your approval. Regularly give your child the chance to be in charge of an activity, even if it's only for a few minutes every day. Let him suggest a game, then join in. He will appreciate your recognition of his ability to draw you in to the delights of his world.

Keep a predictable schedule and daily routines. Knowing that certain events go forward in a predictable manner frees your child from having to guess what's expected of him. For instance, when mealtime always involves sitting in a particular chair, and when dinner is followed by bath time, which is followed by story time and then bedtime, your child will be relaxed enough to follow through with sleep. If, on the other hand, each evening brings its own chaos, your child naturally will want to be involved with each new activity and will not know when it's time to wind down. The need for routine does not preclude spontaneity, of course. If one night's bathtime evolves into a rollicking good time as your child discovers the fun of pouring water from one bucket to another, then let the activity unfold, even if that means getting off schedule. The key is to put daily hallmarks—getting up, dressed and out, eating, bedtime—on automatic pilot so that your child's energies need not be spent trying to figure out each day anew.

In the course of the day, too, you can help your child anticipate the day's events so that he's not left guessing what will happen next. For example, while he's having breakfast, tell him what's in store for the morning. When you're shopping, tell him what kinds of stores he'll see to help him anticipate events rather than being thrown off by unexpected happenings. Also work with your child's body clock. No child, no matter how cooperative he generally is, can be on his best behavior all of the time. For example, if your child tends to get cranky in the afternoon, try to schedule shopping trips for the morning.

Let your child make some choices. While you shouldn't overwhelm your toddler with too many options, choosing between a green bean and a carrot or his red or blue hat will give him the sense of power that he needs. Moreover, by making choices, he can reject the carrot and the blue hat without having to say "No" to eating or getting dressed.

Look for opportunities for cooperation. Being invited to help you do anything that involves movement—picking up toys, carrying a loaf of bread from the store to the car—makes your child burst with pride. It also gives him practice in the art of cooperating and lets him know that he's a valued member of the family team.

Let your child experience the consequences of his actions. Within the bounds of safety and common sense, let your child learn the effects of his actions. Rather than hover over him while you make sure he doesn't spill the food from his bowl, give him just a little at a time and let him find out what will happen if he dumps it on himself. Don't rush to dry him and make him comfortable immediately. Instead, simply say, "Now you're wet. If you don't want to get wet, don't turn over your bowl." If your child tries to lift something that's too heavy, such as your briefcase, don't insist that he not try. He'll figure out soon enough and on his own that it's too heavy. If he doesn't want to put on his shoes, or let you put them on, in order to go outside, simply say, "Let me know when you're ready to put your shoes on so we can go outside." In that way, he doesn't lose face when he opts for the shoes, whereas getting into a struggle with you over wearing them doesn't give him the opportunity to try cooperating rather than resisting. Consequences let your child learn from experience, thus making the learning more meaningful and memorable.

Use language. Because your toddler does not yet have the language skills himself to tell you why he does what he does, you will have to speak for him to see if he agrees with your interpretation of his actions. For example, if you see him reaching for a vase, you might say, "It looks like you want to touch that vase." If he nods to show he understands, you might then explain why he is not allowed to touch the vase, or you could hold the vase for him to touch while explaining that it is not a plaything and can only be handled with your help. If he physically acts out due to anger or frustration, perhaps biting or hitting a playmate, intervene. Help him put words to his feelings. Say, "I know you're angry." Then reinforce what he needs to know in words, "but you are not allowed to bite." (For more, see "Handling aggressive behavior" later in this chapter.)

Set an example. In your actions with your child and with others, show a cooperative spirit. If, for instance, your toddler spills cereal all over the floor, instead of reacting in a confrontational way, saying, "Now look what you've done!" look for ways to involve your child positively. You might say, "Help me clean up. Let's put all the spilled cereal into the trash." Speak kindly to adults, from your spouse to a clerk at the store. When your toddler hears you say something like, "What's wrong with you?" to another, he learns to look for arguments. If, on the other hand, he hears you ask a vendor to please recount the change, he witnesses problem solving in a cooperative manner.

CONFLICT
The need to please you—and himself

Your toddler wants nothing more than to please you—and himself. When you and he want the same things, there's no conflict either with you or within himself. After all, your toddler reasons, anything he wants is good. He is good. You are good. Therefore, if he follows his heart's desires and does what he wants, he (and you, too) will be happy. Of course, that's not always the case. Sometimes you want him to go to sleep when he's more interested in what's going on in the living room. Sometimes you want him to refrain from touching that interesting knob on the CD player. Sometimes you want him to hold your hand while you walk across the playground, but he'd rather run under the swings. The need to reconcile his need to do the things he wants to do with his need for you to share his pleasure (or at least not interfere with it) creates a real crisis for your toddler. The difference between your desires and his creates a gulf between you. It's a necessary gulf, one that helps him define himself as a separate person. But, it's potentially painful and confusing, nonetheless.

Your toddler cannot, as much as part of him would like to, conform to your every wish. Neither can he act on all of his impulses. Some simply will be too difficult. If, for instance, you put him in his car seat, he may not, as hard as he tries, get out. Following other impulses may not be worth it when interesting alternatives are available. For example, if you thwart his attempts to run away in the playground, he may be content to turn his attention to the sandbox, where lots of fun things seem to be happening.

Some impulses are overwhelming, and he follows them without regard to consequences. He might dump out the sugar bowl just to see what happens. He's not at all sure why you're angry. To him, the action is no different from playing with sand at the playground. He's sad and possibly frightened by your displeasure. He may sweep his hands across the table to make the mess disappear, all the while watching you to see if he's regained your good graces. When his actions lead to your need to correct him, he's left with conflicting emotions. How can his good deed lead to a bad response from you? he wonders. He may worry that he has lost your love. He may be afraid that the gulf is wider than it should be. He may climb into your lap just to assure himself that you two remain close and that his separateness from you is not complete.

Your toddler's growing understanding of language serves him well now. Beginning this year, he can respond to verbal reminders and directions. If he approaches the sugar bowl, your "No. Don't touch" will keep him from it long enough for you to remove it from harm's way. Or you may allow him to handle it gently, perhaps letting him feel the texture of the sugar, maybe tasting it. Then your need to prevent a mess and his need to explore are in balance and you avoid a conflict.

Just as you childproof the environment to reduce conflicts, your toddler will look for ways to include you in his explorations to help limit your disapproval—if you're doing something with him, you may be less likely to correct what he is doing. When you're responsive to his body language and speech, and share as much as possible his enthusiasm for all his discoveries, his inner conflicts—as well as his outward conflicts with you—are lessened. Some conflict, however, is inevitable and even desirable, and serves to reinforce your child's sense of himself and appreciation for the differences between the two of you.

How it feels to be me

I am good and lovable. I am powerful. I can do just about everything. I want to be like you. I want to touch what I see, go where I want to go, do what I want, when I want to. Most of the time, when I do something new, you smile at me and tell me what a good thing I've done. But sometimes, when I do something, you frown and tell me "No." I don't always understand what makes you upset. I'm learning that the word *no* is very important, so I will say "No," too. I just want to be loved and to do what I want to do. I get angry when you don't let me have my own way. I get sad when you are angry at me.

YOU AND YOUR CHILD
Understanding your parenting style

How you discipline your child has as much to do with your style of parenting as it does with your child's behavior. If you expect absolute compliance, you're likely to view your toddler's behavior as difficult to manage even when there are no real misbehaviors involved. If you have a laid-back attitude, you may be unconcerned with misbehaviors that others would be less willing to tolerate. Your temperament, your own experiences as a child, and your values play an enormous role in how you discipline and what behaviors you find unacceptable. Your spouse brings all of his or her temperament, experiences, and values to the table, too. It's no wonder that discipline is an issue that concerns parents so much. There simply are so many factors and so many theories on what works and what doesn't that it's difficult to sort it all out. A good place to begin is to look at the broad categories of parenting styles: authoritarian, permissive, and authoritative.

Authoritarian

The authoritarian parent expects obedience without much regard for a child's needs or limitations. While a child of an authoritarian parent may learn to comply to the rules of the home, he will not readily internalize the value of cooperation. He will do what he's told simply to avoid getting in trouble. As he grows, he will comply when he must but will do what he wants when no one is checking on his behavior. He may grow up timid, afraid to act on his own, or he may become defiant, pushing equally hard against reasonable rules as against unreasonable ones. Authoritarian parents depend on their physical presence to enforce the rules and have a difficult time appropriately adjusting the rules as the child grows.

Permissive

When a parent is permissive, he or she lets the child determine much of his behavior. The permissive parent tends to be yielding and inconsistent when it comes to discipline. A permissive parent places few demands on the child. The child's impulses are usually tolerated and rarely punished. This parent spends a great deal of time explaining why a rule is necessary and negotiating for the behavior he or she wants. The parent ends up waiting and wishing the child would behave, or completely giving up and doing nothing. Without boundaries, the child will not feel safe. When given no guidelines on when and how he should control his impulses, he is likely to lose control, which can be frightening. With clear boundaries in place, a child knows what to expect and is provided a secure, steady, and safe environment in which to explore and grow. Learning to live with boundaries helps a child survive and succeed later when he moves into the greater world of school, work, and play. Without boundaries set and enforced early in life, it becomes that much harder for a child to learn the rules he will encounter in the bigger world.

Authoritative

An authoritative parent generally thinks of himself or herself as a guide or a leader, but doesn't think of himself or herself as infallible. While exercising a firm control, an authoritative parent is willing to use reason, negotiation, and conflict resolution to resolve discipline issues. The child is allowed to become independent within set limits and so is encouraged to develop self-discipline. The rights of both child and parent are recognized in the home of authoritative parents. The best outcome for children and parents rests with the authoritative parent, who will assert his or her authority while guiding the child toward morally and socially acceptable behavior in a manner that respects a child's needs.

HELPING YOUR CHILD GROW
Disciplining effectively

In the coming years, disciplining your child will involve sharing your values, teaching right from wrong, and guiding him toward self-discipline. The impulsivity and self-centeredness that accompany his actions now will be tempered by maturity someday. In the meantime, disciplining your toddler involves keeping your child safe and planting the seeds of socially acceptable behavior.

Once you have limited the occasions for misbehavior, it's easier to narrow down the rules you need your child to follow. The appropriate rules for one-year-olds can be broadly termed "Be careful" and "Be nice." Neither of those phrases, however, has any real meaning for your toddler because they are about concepts, not actions. So your teaching will have to be explicit in words and, often, with follow-up actions of your own. For example, you might need to gently hold your child's wrist or arm while saying, "I will not let you hit." Or, while firmly putting your child in a car seat, you can say, "I know you don't want to be in the car seat, but you have it to be safe."

Consistency is vital as you seek to help your child internalize the important rules you've established. To insist, for instance, that he sit in his car seat for every ride and then to allow him to sit in your lap for a short drive will make it that much harder to enforce the car seat rule the next time. To tell him not to grab a toy from a playmate but to ignore the grabbing if the other child seems not to mind will confuse him.

Consistency also pays off when enforcing "quality of life" issues that may not involve safety or social skills but are, nevertheless, essential for keeping your sanity. If, for example, you don't want him to play with the telephone, you must (if you can't simply put the phone where he can't reach it) correct him or redirect his attention each time he grabs for it. If, on the other hand, you tell him not to touch the telephone and scold him again and again for doing so, but then decide to ignore the behavior, your child will need to test your response. He will continue to play with it until you've reestablished the rule or he has lost interest in the phone.

Changing the rules as your child grows is a necessary step in your child's maturing process. In most cases, your child will give you clues that a rule needs adjusting. He may attempt to climb over a stair gate, demonstrating his improved dexterity—and letting you know that it may be time to allow him easier access to the stairs. Just as he grabbed the spoon from you to show you that he could feed himself, his insistence on doing something that once was a no-no may indicate that he's ready for a change.

If you feel it is time to change the limits and let your child do some things he hasn't been permitted to do before, make sure you let him know. If you don't, he may become confused or even scared when you ignore his doing something that you had previously prohibited. Saying something like "Now that you're bigger, I'm going to let you climb the stairs" acknowledges that he has grown, and you give him a sense of accomplishment and capability.

For less clear-cut issues, don't be afraid to back off and give your child some leeway. While he angrily squirms away from a needed diaper change, you can say, "I see that you really don't want to be changed right now," and let him continue to play, while warning, "I'll have to change your diaper soon." He may then willingly go along.

Dealing with common misbehaviors

Handling typical toddler "crimes and misdemeanors" does not depend on punishments or lengthy lectures. These are best dealt with by firmness and consistency delivered swiftly and in an authoritative tone. Since your child wants very much to please you—and to avoid displeasing you—your voice and your stance are your best tools for attracting his attention and gaining his cooperation. When you need to correct your toddler, use a serious tone, while gearing your body language to match. For example, you could frown, put your hands on your hips, and look directly at your child while saying, "I get angry when you throw things on the floor." Or "I am really upset that you dumped out that drawer." Using such "I" messages will also convey the message that it's the actions and not the person that causes you distress. Following are the usual toddler activities that need your response and suggested discipline strategies:

Running off. When your toddler takes off in an unsafe area such as a parking lot, he's completely unaware of the danger. When you catch him, tell him sternly that he cannot run away from you. Give him a chance to walk alongside you, but if he begins to take off again, repeat your warning and hold him, even if he struggles. If necessary, restrain him in a stroller. Respond to his anger by making eye contact and repeating that he cannot run off. Make sure, too, that when he has opportunities to run safely, he knows running is allowed there. Be explicit: "You can run in the park because the fence will keep you from going too far."

Ignoring "No." When your child repeats an unacceptable behavior and ignores your reminders to stop, you'll have to reinforce your words with actions, such as physically removing him from the scene, perhaps placing him in his high chair while you tell him why he's being corrected. You might say, "I need for you to listen. You touched the stove after I told you not to. Now you'll have to sit here." Limit the "time out" to just a minute or so. Then, when giving him his freedom, remind him that if he touches the stove again, you'll have to put him back in his chair. Follow through.

Screaming and screeching. Your toddler's natural exuberance can often include high noise levels. Much of the time, you can ignore the decibel level. But if his playful screaming gets to be too much or if he is disturbing others, such as in a crowded elevator, you'll have to quiet him down. Redirect his energy by asking him a question, whispering something to him, or inviting him to sing with you. Since he loves what his voice can do, teach him to whisper. If he's yelling out of anger, quietly say, "I can't understand you when you're so loud. Please speak softly so I can understand." Don't join in a shouting match, which won't teach him the value of quiet.

Dealing with tantrums

The best way to deal with tantrums is to prevent them. Though they often seem to come out of the blue, most tantrums have a definable cause. If your toddler is given to tantrums, pay attention to when he has them, including time of day, whether they occur before or after a meal or a specific event, and circumstances surrounding it, such as being restricted, frustrated, hungry, or overtired. Once you're able to identify your child's tantrum triggers, you may be able to eliminate many of them.

If your toddler is subject to meltdowns when schedules become erratic, adhere more strictly to a daily routine. Make sure that he takes naps and eats meals at the same time every day. Set regular routines and times for baths and bedtime. Also be sure that your child has plenty of opportunities to explore without being thwarted by "Nos" at every turn.

Some toddlers lapse into tantrums when they are overtired or hungry. Try to stick to a regular sleep routine so your toddler gets enough sleep. Be sure to carry snacks with you when you go out, and don't wait until the tantrum is about to happen before you offer the food or try to get your child to rest.

Anticipate situations in which your child may become overly frustrated. While still providing challenges, don't involve your toddler in activities that are too difficult for his stage of development. And when you see that an activity is about to become too frustrating, offer help, asking, "Would you like me to help you?" rather than stepping in and taking over. Don't put enticing items or activities in front of your toddler that he is not allowed to touch or use. For example, don't walk him past the playground if your schedule won't allow you to let him have some time on the swings.

There are times, of course, when, in spite of your best planning and sensitivity to your child's needs, his behavior erupts into a full-blown tantrum. When a tantrum does strike, there are things you can do to minimize it.

Stay calm. If you become upset, you will only make it harder for your child to calm down. Now, when he's out of control, he needs you to be in control.

Talk quietly. A quiet voice tells your toddler that even though his tantrum scares him, it doesn't scare you. And if he wants to hear what you are saying, he will have to calm down and refocus his energies to hear you.

Don't try to reason or argue with your toddler in the midst of a tantrum. While he's upset, he won't be able to comprehend anything you have to say. Limit your words to reassurances that you're going to help him calm down.

Contain him. Hold him closely if he's flailing, which will keep him from hurting himself or others and may give him the sense of security he needs to help to dissolve the anger. If you cannot hold him, move him to a safe place, such as his crib, the sofa, or his stroller. Don't leave him alone, however; that will only increase his terror.

Try to distract your child. Before a tantrum reaches full pitch or as it's on the wane, try to redirect his attention. There's often no need to stay focused on the tantrum and some toddlers will be dissuaded from a meltdown by something new.

Ignore the outburst. Say, "I don't like the way you're acting," and then go about your business. You might hum or sing as you go to make it clear that you are paying no attention. Your child may get worse for a while, but when he receives no reaction from you, he may give up wasting so much energy. This method is not recommended if your child is overly sensitive or is going through a difficult time. In a case such as this, comforting him may be more effective.

Don't pay attention to what others think. If you're in public, try not to be intimidated by any audience you may attract. Remember that tantrums are a normal part of a toddler's behavior and anyone who has had a toddler knows that.

Don't give in. It can be tempting to give your child what he wants to short circuit a tantrum, but that's a bad precedent to start. If you can prevent a tantrum by giving your child something he's allowed to have, by all means, do so. But if you have a reason for denying him what he wants, don't let the fear of a tantrum sway you.

Handling aggressive behavior

Toddlers may act aggressively—hitting, biting, pushing, pulling hair, or grabbing—for a number of reasons, none of which stem from a desire to do harm to others. However, since their actions can indeed be hurtful, it's important to instill the rules of social behavior early. One-year-olds misbehave in this manner out of frustration, because they can't express themselves yet in words, and out of simple curiosity. For instance, a toddler knows that biting a peach is a good thing and wonders what it might be like to bite your arm. When you stop him from climbing onto the lamp table, he may hit you because that's more within his ability than to say, "I'm really angry at you for stopping me." When he pushes a child out of the way, too, that's his way of saying, "You're too close." Even though his reasons may be understandable, you need to help him control these impulses and to begin to guide him toward empathy. When your child engages in such activities, never react in kind by biting or hitting so that he "knows what it feels like." At age one, he cannot make the connection between what he did and why you're suddenly hurting him. All he'll remember of this lesson is that his parent who usually protects him is now causing him harm.

Instead, as with other misbehaviors, react sternly and swiftly. Do not allow him to hit or bite. Say, "I know you're angry, but you cannot hit" or "Biting is not allowed. Biting hurts." If he does the same again, remove him from the situation, telling him why. "I can't allow you to hit, so I'm putting you where you can't hit."

This age is too soon to insist on any form of apology, such as having your child say, "I'm sorry." You can, however, demonstrate approaching whomever he hurt gently and showing your child more appropriate ways to interact.

Teaching social skills

Getting along with others, and treating adults and other children kindly and with respect, is a tall order for a one-year-old. However, now is the time to initiate training about certain social rules.

Sharing and taking turns. Rarely will a one-year-old willingly share his possessions or patiently wait in line for his turn at the slide. However, he can begin to learn these concepts this year. When arranging play times with other toddlers, try to have duplicate toys on hand so that neither child feels compelled to grab the other's. Talk about sharing and turn taking. Play practice games, such as rolling a ball back and forth while noting, "Now it's my turn to have the ball. Now it's your turn." Ask to see a toy of his. Offer to show him something interesting of yours in return. For example, say, "May I hold your truck? Would you like to hold my keys?"

Politeness. Using the words *please* and *thank you* when talking with your child and offering reminders to do so himself will help your toddler absorb these basic rules of politeness. But don't insist that he say please every time he asks for something. You might simply note, "I like it when you say please." To teach him public manners, play games that show expected behavior. For instance, before going to a (child-friendly) restaurant, play restaurant at home. For the actual visit, be sure to have quiet toys and other distractions available to keep him pleasantly occupied for the benefit of other diners.

Waiting. Toddlers can't wait patiently. Putting your child in a position in which he has to wait—such as when you meet a friend on the street and wish to talk for a moment—can help him develop a habit of impatient whining and pulling at you. But it's not a good idea to excuse yourself from socializing because your child is insisting that you do so. Your best response is to be prepared so that both your need to socialize and his need to keep going are satisfied. For instance, if you keep distractions packed in your pocket, you can produce something interesting for your child to examine while you enjoy your chat. You can also put into words what you're doing: "I'd like to talk to my friend now, so you can play with my keys while I'm talking." You may not be able to keep him distracted for a half hour, but by allowing yourself some time with your friend, you've accomplished two things: you've given yourself some much-needed adult company, and you've given your child the opportunity to learn that you have a right to focus your attention someplace other than him now and then.

Getting away from "No"

Parents of one-year-olds—and one-year-olds themselves—are well acquainted with the word *no*. It's useful, easy to say, and often the most effective barrier between your child and harm's way. But like anything else, it can begin to lose its power if it's overused. To reduce the use of "No," try these strategies:

Use "No" only when you have to. When the situation concerns immediate threats to safety, health, and your sanity, it is appropriate to say "No." Substitute words like "hot" or "dangerous" when you see your child approaching something he shouldn't but when he is not yet in any particular danger.

Don't use "No" to stop your child from his natural inclination to explore. Whenever possible, turn a "No" into a positive, saying something like, "I see that you want to reach the glass on the table. Would you like me to show it to you?" Then supervise his handling of the item. Instead of saying, "Don't walk near the street," rephrase it as "Walk on the sidewalk where it's safe."

Never plead or make your "No" sound like a request. When you say "No," mean it.

When your child does comply with "No," make sure to thank him. As always, good behavior should be acknowledged.

Discipline strategies that work

For your toddler to learn the safety and social rules he needs to learn, your immediate show of displeasure—a stern look and a serious tone of voice—is highly effective. Physical intervention along with your verbal correction—removing a sand tosser from the sandbox or gently constraining a hitter—also reinforces your message that certain activities are not permitted.

Positive attention also helps your child develop the cooperative spirit that is the hallmark of a well-disciplined person. When your toddler handles his teddy bear gently, you can let him know that he's doing a good thing: "I think your bear must be happy because you're handling it so gently." When he allows you to dress him easily, let him know you appreciate it: "Thanks for being so helpful while I got you dressed." When he's let go of a misbehavior, thank him for that, too. "I liked it when you stopped running when I called you."

Your firm and consistent reminders to follow the rules will, eventually, lead your child to self-discipline and the ability to make moral choices when he is old enough to do so.

Do punishments work?

Punishment doesn't have a place in the life of a one-year-old. Spanking, even hand slapping, gives the wrong message to a child who's busy learning how the world works by imitating the actions of the adults who matter to him. All that a slap teaches him is that the adults who usually are gentle with him sometimes hurt him. He's unable to make the connection between his misbehavior and your reaction. Time outs, which can be effective with older kids, rely on a more sophisticated understanding of cause and effect than a young toddler is capable of absorbing. Denial of privileges, too, a strategy that can work with older children, is not useful with toddlers.

The people I know

Your toddler's relationships with family, friends, and others

At the beginning of your child's second year, she was full of smiles and giggles when a familiar face approached. Smiling strangers, too, may have animated your 12-month-old and made her burst with delight at the attention. Somewhere around 18 months, however, she may begin to turn away from anyone but you. She's likely to prefer one parent (usually Mom) to the other, especially in times of crisis. In her relationships with adults she knows well, she sees you and others as helpmates, there to soothe a hurt or supply a needed item. If she has a regular caregiver other than you, she will readily accept and rely on that person though she is aware that she doesn't share the same intense bond with the caregiver as she does with you.

During this year, your toddler notices other children as never before and watches them intently, even if she's not always willing to join them in their play. Siblings and pets garner strong interest, though grandparents and other relatives who are not part of daily life may inspire more alarm than calm. She's interested in socializing, especially when it complements her need for mobility and practicing language skills. However, her lack of social skills will result in some hurt feelings for herself and her playmates.

Ironically, as she moves further from you, a great benefit of her increased mobility, she becomes more clingy much of the time, and may be downright hysterical if you leave her in the care of others. This year, dealing with separation anxiety—both hers and your own—will be a major challenge. As she approaches age two and her sense of time as well as her language skills improve, she will be better able to understand that losing sight of you does not mean losing you forever.

DEVELOPMENTAL MILESTONE
Your child's awareness of others

If you drew a circle to represent your toddler's world at the beginning of this year, you would have to place her right in the middle. She is at the center and all others revolve around her. She knows other people exist, especially her parents and other close family members, but she does not yet have any real concept of them as separate people. As far as she is concerned, they think and feel the same as she does. Their purpose is to entertain her and to meet her physical and emotional needs.

Between the ages of one and two, your child will go through phases when she seems to ignore you and other people completely, except when she wants something. She may seem to have lost all of the cuddly affection she showed you when she was a baby, except when she is tired and wants to be held. As little attention as she pays to you, she will still interact more with you than she will with other adults or children. Her biggest concern, clearly, is interacting with her environment, not necessarily the people in it. When around other children, she may seem to treat them almost as she would when exploring furniture or other objects. She may poke at them or pull their hair and be fascinated when they react. She may bump into or even walk over a playmate to get to something else she finds interesting.

Gradually, during the second half of the year, your child will begin to understand that other people are different from her and have feelings just as she does. She will develop an interest in other children and enjoy being around them, while still not actively playing with them for any sustained periods. Play, at this point, is more of a side-by-side operation rather than a real one-on-one interaction. As she comes closer to her second birthday, you will see signs that she wants to cooperate with other children and involve them in her play. And, as she gains language skills, she will begin to want to tell you and others about what she is seeing and doing, a clear sign that she's now aware that others don't always know what she's thinking.

As her awareness of herself as an individual grows, she will be startled and a bit frightened to discover that you are separate from her as she is from you. It's at this point that she enters a period of see-sawing between pushing you away and clinging to you in an effort to assure herself that the separateness is not permanent. When you, not she, is the one to initiate the separation, she may be overwhelmed by anxiety.

Social milestones
Your child's reactions to other people go through distinct phases this year:

12 months. Around the time of her first birthday, your toddler will still like people in general, although she may reveal signs of stranger anxiety. She will show affection to those with whom she's comfortable and will act out in both negative and positive ways to get your attention. She will love to play simple, interactive games. However, most of her time will be spent on physical activities rather than social ones.

15 months. She will become more negative and resist doing things with others. She will probably be happy to play by herself some of the time, although she will expect you to be nearby in case she wants something. Even though she may be less openly affectionate, she will be learning what effect she has on you and others by doing nice things, such as hugging and talking, and things that aren't so nice, such as screaming and hitting. She will be more and more interested in what you do. She'll watch you as you move about the house and try to imitate your actions. And when she acquires a new skill, she will want you to give her your full attention and show your approval for her performance.

18 months. Her negative behavior will peak. She will still be attached to you, yet more resistant than ever to your demands. She will talk more and more, but have difficulty making herself understood, which will lead to frustration. Little by little, she will try to involve others more in her play. However, she may prefer playing with adults to playing with other children. Her interest in adults does not extend to feeling comfortable with those who are not part of her inner sanctum. She may be anxious around people that she does not see regularly. And she may suffer separation anxiety from you even when left in the care of someone whom she knows quite well.

21 months. She will claim her toys with a loud "Mine!" Because she is so possessive of her own things, she will be interested in who owns what. She may be possessive of your belongings, too, and may react strongly if, for instance, your spouse sits in a chair that is usually yours. Likewise, if you are affectionate to others, she'll react jealously, trying to insert herself between you and others, even your spouse. At this point, your toddler also begins to reach out to other children while playing, but she still prefers playing with adults.

24 months. She is much more aware of her separateness from adults and other children. She will enjoy playing with older siblings and imitating them. She will also interact more with other toddlers and fight less as her language skills improve. She will be more willing to cooperate and be eager to please.

How it feels to be me

If I can hold it and touch it, it's mine. That goes for this spoon I'm playing with, and you. If anyone tries to take this spoon away from me, I'll hold on to it with all my might, just as I wouldn't let anyone take away my hand or any other part of me. If I wander away from you, it's okay because I can go back whenever I want. But when you leave me, I feel really scared. What if you never come back?

When I'm doing all sorts of neat things like walking and climbing and reaching for things, I know that I am powerful and important. But when things happen that I don't control, I feel very small and I forget that I am powerful. As long as you're close to me, I can keep figuring out how much I can do. When I see you leaving me, I forget everything except that I don't want you to go.

Age two. You can begin to help your child learn social skills. But don't expect any consistent results for at least another year. Right now, your toddler's only incentive to behave in socially acceptable ways is to please you. Before she adopts social skills as a means of getting along with others, she needs to be certain of her separateness. Likewise, she needs to learn that the separateness she enjoys is the same that you and other people she encounters experience.

CONFLICT
The need for—and fear of—separateness

By the time your toddler is about 18 months old, she will have reached the milestone of understanding her existence as a separate individual, which will cause her to feel both powerful and vulnerable. To compensate for her feelings of vulnerability, she will begin to fiercely hang on to anything she considers hers, from toys to even you. To her, you all belong to her and support her identity. If she sees another child, including a sibling, playing with her possessions or sees you reach out lovingly to another person, she will grow jealous and ready to defend what she believes is hers.

Her inability to share you or her possessions is an attempt on her part to prevent any encroachment on her identity. During this year, her sensitivity toward others and allowance for their separateness will increase, but, in the meantime, she's prepared to battle anyone who threatens her sense of self. Part of defining herself as a separate person rests with her ability to move away from you at will. As long as she's leading this particular dance, she's comfortable with the distance she puts between herself and you. However, when you prove your own separateness by moving freely away from her, she's likely to panic.

Separation anxiety
Separation anxiety is common among one-year-olds, and though it may seem like regressive behavior—acting more babyish than her bursts of independence make her out to be—fear of separation

marks a milestone in your child's emotional and intellectual life. Unlike during her infancy and early toddlerhood, your child now knows that you continue to exist even when she can't see you. When you leave, she feels left out and abandoned. Her ability to imagine you elsewhere without her is not balanced by an ability to imagine you returning.

Separation anxiety can range from mild to extreme. Your child's level of anxiety is not a reflection of the strength of your relationship with her. Rather it's a result of a combination of factors—her temperament, her prior experiences with separation, even how she's feeling physically at the moment. Reactions to anxiety may include clinging, clutching, and loud wails of protest, or may simply be quiet withdrawal.

Her developing memory and intellect allows your toddler to use previous experience to predict when a separation is about to occur. For example, when she sees you in the kitchen preparing food, she knows that she will eat soon. Likewise, when she sees you put on a coat or pick up your car keys, or when another caretaker arrives, she knows you are going to leave the house. Because you are the main star in her orbit, when you leave, it upsets her world tremendously.

If your child is upset when you're about to go...

Do say	Don't say
"I know you're upset. I will be back after lunch."	"Don't feel sad. I don't want to leave, but I have to."
"While I'm gone, you'll play and then you'll have a nap."	"I'm going to miss you so much."
"I'm going now."	"Maybe I can wait just a few more minutes until you calm down."

Helping your child cope with separations

Faced with a crying, obviously distressed child as you are about to go out the door can make any possibility of a solution seem remote. However, there are ways to approach this anxiety that should make the separation easier for both of you:

Have practice runs. Experiencing separations and reunions helps your child understand that separations aren't forever. Before getting your child into any routine in which separations are an everyday occurrence (such as when she begins day care), practice short separations. Leave her in another's care for five to fifteen minutes. Little by little, stretch out the length of your absence.

Expect changes in your child's reactions. At age one, your child might show little concern when left in the care of another. At 18 months, however, she may suddenly begin to howl at the slightest hint of separation. Her new reaction, though it may look like regression, is actually an indication of her growing awareness. With time and patience, she will again be able to handle putting some time and space between the two of you.

Be matter-of-fact in your leave taking. Don't hover, linger, or share any distress of your own. Acknowledge your child's feelings and leave her with a warm hug. Be sure to greet your child's caregiver in a friendly manner, demonstrating your comfort and trust in this person.

Develop leave-taking routines so that your child knows what to expect. Leave yourself plenty of time before you go out so that you aren't rushing at the last minute and have no time for your good-bye ritual. If you have a window that faces the street or the driveway, have your child wave to you from there if that seems to help her. Experiment to understand what routines work best for your child.

Use language to help her understand. Twenty minutes or so before the arrival of a caregiver or before dropping your child off at day care, tell your child what she can expect, mentioning what you'll be doing and what she will be doing. If she's 18 months or older, she'll understand the passage of time through routines. Use her regular activities as time markers, saying, for instance, "I'll be back after you've had your nap." This will be more meaningful than such phrases as "later" or "soon." You might also choose a farewell phrase that you always use, such as "See you later, alligator."

Make your separations as consistent as possible. For example, if your child goes to day care, try as much as possible to take her there and pick her up at the same time every day. Having different routines every day may elongate the time your child needs to learn to deal with separation.

Have comforting and distracting items on hand. If your child has a love object, such as a favorite blankie that she uses to calm herself, make sure it's available. Consider introducing a new toy or activity before leaving so that your child and her caregiver can become involved over a new item after you leave. Don't assume that either will keep her from having a meltdown, however.

Never sneak away. It may seem easier to slip out while your child is distracted, but doing so will only increase her anxiety in the long run and make it harder for her to learn to cope. Let her see you go, while reassuring her quickly that she is in good hands. An obvious exception to this rule is when you're going out in the evening, after your child has already gone to sleep. In that case, however, it's essential that you've chosen a caregiver with whom your child is familiar and comfortable so that, if she does awaken while you're gone, she won't be doubly alarmed by the appearance of a stranger.

Don't scold or tease your child for her reaction. Saying something like "You're a big girl, now" only serves to confuse a child who's feeling vulnerable at the moment.

Trust your child. Have confidence in your child that she can learn to handle necessary separations. Don't undermine her own confidence by sharing in her sadness and anxiety.

Accept your child's reunion style. As wonderful as they are, homecomings can be as challenging as departures. When you return from a separation, your child may run happily to you and want to be picked up. Or she may start crying. Or she may completely ignore you as she emotionally regroups. All styles are normal. The important thing is to accept that the reunion may be as difficult a transition as the parting and to be patient with your child's reactions.

Your child's relationships

This year, your child's relationships will broaden to include not only her immediate family and regular caregiver, if she has one, but others with whom she has less regular contact. She will become aware of the relationships of other people, too. For instance, she may recognize the parent of a playmate and even ask about the playmate when she sees the parent. She knows that they belong together and is a bit disconcerted when she sees the parent without the child in tow. If, when running errands with you to the supermarket, she usually encounters a particular friendly cashier, she may begin to look for that person as soon as you enter the store together. These relationships with others are fleeting, however. Her focus remains on the family.

Making different connections to Mom and Dad

Even as an infant, your child had a different response to you than she did to your spouse. She looked to her primary caregiving parent for nurturing and sustenance. Her relationship with her other parent may have become one of "otherness." There was great excitement surrounding the appearance of the other parent, a chance for something new, a different way of being held, cared for, and entertained.

As a one-year-old, your child continues to experience each parent for his or her unique contributions to meeting her needs and wants. Because her reliance on her primary caregiver for comfort is paramount, she may choose the parent with whom she spends most of her day over the other whenever she's tired or in particular need of reassurance. She will switch her attention to the other for fun and for a new audience for all of her blossoming skills.

Because she has claimed one parent as her primary source of comfort, she may act negatively at times to the other, trying to get between parents when they are close or fighting to get into the arms of the primary caregiver whenever a crisis, including simply being tired, erupts.

Sibling relationships

Toddlers recognize immediately that their older siblings are special people. They see their older siblings as extensions of their parents and, therefore, as sources of help and entertainment. One-year-olds readily attempt to do what their older siblings do and are not particularly bothered when their lower skill level does not allow them to mimic all of their big sister or brother's actions. Largely, this is because older siblings quite naturally adjust their play styles to allow their toddler sibs to interact with them in a more even way. If, for instance, your toddler wants to join your six-year-old playing with a soccer ball, your older child would (if no better player was around) roll the ball gently, giving his littler sibling a chance to play along. If your six-year-old had a peer playmate around, however, he'd most likely call for you to cart the interloping toddler away from the action. You should pull your toddler away from the game as the older children aren't likely to remember to be careful. Being kept away from the game will fuel your toddler's frustration and will result in her fury, so you should try to distract her with another activity.

When a younger sibling arrives, your toddler may show a great deal of interest and will want a chance to touch and handle the new baby, just as she would show an interest in any new object. She will naturally assume that the baby is hers (after all, everything else is, in her mind) and will feel possessive toward the newcomer. She will also feel jealous of the baby's place in your lap and will probably insist that you make room for her, too. Better yet, from her point of view, would be to send the baby back to wherever it came from once she's satisfied her interest and wants to move on to other things. Any strong reaction against your new arrival will lessen over a relatively brief time. Once again, her lack of an ability to understand time will work in her favor and she will soon forget what life was like before the new baby. The jealousy she feels will be in the present, existing only when the baby literally comes between the two of you. In general, the new addition to your family will be a source of interest some of the time and an object not worthy of her attention at other times.

Toddler friendships
Friendships among toddlers are quite different than the friendships based on similar interests that will form later in your child's life. Right now, friendships are side-by-side events, in which your toddler will enjoy the proximity of another child much as she enjoys a toy that makes noises and performs movements. Because she is becoming aware of the separateness of herself from you and her possessions, however, she will, as the year goes on, look at other toddlers with a growing understanding that they are like her and have ideas that are different from her own.

While your toddler still prefers grown-ups as playmates, other toddlers offer your child new ways of learning. Toddlers will eye one another's play style and mimic one another's actions. Because they intuitively know that they are alike in terms of size and skill level, toddlers encourage one another to experience feelings based on others' feelings. For instance, if one toddler laughs, her play-mate may laugh simply as a way of announcing, "I'm noticing you." Likewise, when a playmate cries, your toddler may burst into tears in sympathy. She may even display the beginnings of empathy by attempting to make her playmate feel better by gently patting her arm or by offering a toy. Of course, she may a moment later cause new tears by grabbing the toy back and will not recognize that her own behavior was the source of her friend's sadness.

Friendships among toddlers encourage language development because, unlike you, your toddler's playmate will not recognize what she is saying. Your child will have to struggle to find words that will be meaningful to her playmate. The word *mine,* of course, will surface frequently. Each child's sensitivity to body language will also be part of her communication lesson. Your child will learn, for instance, that getting too close to a playmate may result in being pushed, or that holding a toy out is a gesture that means, "Do you want to see it?" Because toddlers know that people inter-act with language, they may exchange their newfound word-mak-ing skills for babbling with one another, producing the cadences of speech but without needing to be understood or to understand.

YOU AND YOUR CHILD
Sharing the caring

There's a certain comfort for a parent in knowing that he or she alone can satisfy a child's needs at the moment. It's a confirmation that your importance to your child is as central to her as it is to you. But there's a subtle danger in allowing your child's preference for you at times to get between her and her other parent or between her and other relatives and caregivers.

To broaden your child's circle to include others who care for her does not diminish your own important role in her life. Nor does it lessen the intensity of your relationship with your child. On the contrary, when you let go of playing the part of a gatekeeper, monitoring and directing how other caring people interact with your child, you free yourself and your child to enjoy far richer relationships. If, for example, you assume that your child will be absolutely fine in the care of your spouse, your relationship with your spouse is certainly enhanced. Moreover, your spouse's confidence in parenting your child grows, feeding your child's sense of self-worth and helping her to develop her own intense relationship with her other parent. In addition, your child benefits from your spouse's different manner of handling her. However, if you're anxious about your child's safety and comfort when you separate from her or you hover when your spouse does his or her part in child care, you drive a wedge between you and your spouse. By playing the role of the better, more competent, parent, you undermine your spouse's confidence in his or her parenting abilities, and cut your child off from another source of comfort.

Likewise, when leaving your child in the care of a caregiver, whether a professional sitter, your parents, or another trusted adult, your child will benefit from your calm trust in that person and will learn, by watching your reactions, if her own anxiety is well founded. If, on the other hand, you linger a bit too long or constantly reassure your child that you'll be back soon, you intensify her anxiety.

HELPING YOUR CHILD GROW
Enhancing your child's relationships
Even though central casting has placed you as the star in your child's life, your other role this year is to facilitate your toddler's ability to form relationships with other players in this drama.

Your child's other parent
You can help enhance this important relationship by supporting his or her unique parenting style, recognizing that "different" doesn't mean either superior or inferior. If you find yourself anxious about relinquishing your director's role in your child's life, ask yourself honestly why it's important to you to be in charge.

If your spouse works outside the home and your primary work is raising your child, do you feel that your spouse is infringing on your turf by sharing in the parenting responsibilities? Or if you work away from home and leave your child in the care of others, do you feel that you have to be in charge whenever you're available? Try to see that it's in your child's benefit to have two involved parents who each offer your child something the other cannot.

Are you afraid that your partner lacks the expertise to do things correctly? Then recognize that the day-to-day experience of helping to raise your child is the best means of gaining that needed competence. In a manner that suggests cooperation rather than confrontation, you might also offer books and articles that address any areas of concern so that your spouse can see on what basis you're forming your child-rearing principles.

On the other hand, you may want your child's other parent to take a more active role than he or she is currently taking. How can you draw him or her in? Again, a spirit of cooperation rather than confrontation is your best bet. Be sure that you're not using time spent with your child to measure equality within your relationship with your spouse. It is possible for each partner to be making a significant, though different, contribution to the family. In fact, it's likely that one parent will be more actively involved than the other, a situation that is fine for your toddler as long as each parent has a chance to develop his or her own relationship with her.

Make sure that the family schedule encourages shared one-on-one time—even 15 minutes a day or a few hours a week—when your partner can enjoy your child's company alone. Don't interfere with how they spend that time. If your child balks at being separated from you, you need not always honor her preference. Saying something like "Daddy wants to hold you now" matter-of-factly sends the message to your toddler that both her parents are competent caregivers. Make sure, too, that you're not sending mixed messages, asking for more involvement while questioning his or her competence by stepping in, taking over, or criticizing.

Each partner needs to make a conscious decision to accept the other's unique way of sharing time with your toddler. If, for example, your child returns from an outing with your spouse covered in chocolate ice cream, you could either show your upset at the mess or make a comment like, "It looks like you two had a great time." The former would undermine the growing relationship while the latter would put the value of the relationship over the value of your child's outfit. Share books and magazine articles that stress the importance of each parent's contribution to child rearing.

By far the most important way to encourage a strong bond between your child and her other parent is to demonstrate a strong relationship between her parents. When your child regularly witnesses her mother and father acting lovingly (even though she may exhibit jealously) toward one another, she develops a sense of security that will enhance her relationships with you and with others.

Enhancing sibling relationships

Siblings share genes, parents, space, and many experiences. That does not mean, however, that they share the same play style, have the same needs, or respond in the same ways to your parenting style or other situations.

To help your toddler develop a good rapport with an older sibling:

Don't put your older child in charge of the younger one. While it can boost an older child's self-esteem to be asked to entertain a toddler sibling for a few minutes, putting one sibling "in charge" of the other is not a good idea. Your older child may, at age three, four, five, or even twelve, seem mature when compared to your toddler. However, he does not have the maturity to handle a toddler's physical or emotional safety. If your older child is much older, don't take for granted that he will baby-sit or entertain his sibling on a regular basis. If he volunteers, show your gratitude.

Honor your older child's attachment to his possessions. If your older child has outgrown a toy that you think would be appropriate for your toddler, suggest that he pass it down. Don't just take things without permission. When your older one does give things to your toddler, praise the generosity. Likewise, an older child needs to feel that he is not alone in protecting his possessions. An older child needs you on his side to keep a toddler from damaging his stuff.

Respect your older child's immaturity and limitations. Don't expect your older child to be responsible for keeping the peace between his younger sibling and himself. Telling an older child to give in to a toddler sibling's demands simply because he is older isn't fair and builds resentment. Likewise, don't expect your older child to always remember to safeguard your toddler or to safeguard his possessions. For instance, if your six-year-old leaves his blocks where your toddler can get them, it's appropriate to remind the older one of the need to keep small toys out of the toddler's reach. You can follow up frequent reminders by limiting your older child's access to the blocks for a short time. However, childproofing for your toddler's safety remains your responsibility. No older sibling should feel that it's up to him to ensure a toddler's well-being.

Make sure your older child enjoys the perks that come with his older status. Though your toddler may want all the things and privileges of her older sibling, your older one has earned certain considerations that your toddler has not. For instance, if your five-year-old is beginning kindergarten and you buy him a backpack and school supplies, you need not do the same for your toddler. Your older child deserves his special moments and will appreciate your acknowledgment of his own status. Let your older child stay up later or have some other appropriate privilege, too.

Find ways to safeguard your older child's privacy. Make sure your older one has time alone and time alone with you.

Help your older child understand your toddler's moods. You may find, at times, that your older child wants very much to play with your toddler, but your toddler is not at all interested. The older one, used to being the leader, may be quite upset to find that his younger sibling has a mind of her own and doesn't want to play his games. Your toddler is more than likely rejecting one more boss in her drive to become independent. So, as well as you can, explain the situation to your older child. You might also suggest activities they could do together, in the side-by-side manner that pleases toddlers, such as playing with clay, playing with blocks, or drawing pictures. If your older child knows how to read, you could also suggest that he read a story to his little sibling.

For a child whose world revolves around herself, the entrance of a baby who commands much of your attention can be a real jolt. To smooth the transition from being the youngest family member to an older sibling:

Be prepared for a range of reactions. Don't expect that your toddler either will be enthralled or horrified by the arrival of a sibling. She may be curious and happy one moment and angry and jealous the next. She may even be thoroughly uninterested. Don't insist that she get to know the baby right away, but don't keep them apart unnecessarily either. When the baby makes different sounds, you might ask your toddler if she thinks the baby is hungry, needs a nap, or just wants some attention. You can also offer to let her hold the baby by setting her in a chair, then placing the baby in her arms with plenty of support.

Don't add other changes, if possible. While you may not be able to delay or hurry a move to a new house so that it doesn't occur right when you bring home a sibling, keeping other changes to a minimum is a good idea. If your toddler will start day care, begin a few weeks before or after your baby's homecoming. Don't move her out of her room, her place in your bed, or her crib right now so that she doesn't feel displaced. If the new baby will be using your newborn's outgrown bouncy chair, clothing, or bottles, remove them from your toddler's life a few months before the baby arrives. Asking her, for instance, to turn over her baby chair that she now uses for her dolls to the new baby will bring out your toddler's natural possessiveness.

Expect some regression. Your toddler may have given up her pacifier or bottle, but if she sees the baby to whom you're giving so much attention enjoy these things, she may want them again. You can handle her need for babyish behavior while encouraging her continued drive to maturity by drawing on her new appreciation for make-believe. You might say, "You want to pretend to be a baby. It's okay to pretend," and let her act the part now and then.

Help your toddler appreciate her own special place. Let your toddler look at pictures of herself when she was a baby. Ask her how she's changed. Help her put into words the skills she's gained: "You can walk now, but when you were a baby, you couldn't walk. The baby can't walk yet either." Don't make too big a deal, however, about how helpful she can be. While some toddlers may occasionally like being a helper, handing you a diaper or singing to their baby sister or brother, some would rather not. By emphasizing her ability to help, your toddler may feel pressured to do so and disappointed that she can't do it on her own terms. If your toddler is not interested in helping, don't push her into doing so. Also be careful not to give her responsibility she can't handle, which may endanger the baby. And never leave the two of them alone together, even for a few seconds.

Be sure to give your toddler one-on-one time with you. When she understands that you will still have time for her, she will be reassured.

Planting the seeds of friendship

Your child's temperament will determine how readily she takes to making friends with other children. If your child has always been social, smiling easily at people and enjoying social settings, she may eagerly greet another toddler with smiles and hugs. If she takes time to warm up to people, she may warm to another child with a quiet demeanor once she's had a chance to observe her for a time.

How do you know your child has a friend? Generally, the most obvious sign is that your child prefers a particular child over other children. She may greet this special playmate with great happiness and glee. Even when they are not together, your child may say her friend's name and show happiness thinking about the playmate. You can watch for less obvious signs when your child is with her friend. Instead of being involved only with parallel play, toddlers who are drawn to one another will purposely do things together, such as playing with toys in the same way and imitating each other in various activities. To communicate with one another, toddler friends may rely more on gestures and babbles rather than on any of the real words they have learned.

Helping your toddler play with others

At this age, playdates for your child are nice additions to her social life, but not essential. If your child is currently not in day care or involved in play groups, don't worry that she will be at any disadvantage as she enters her preschool years. Although your child will enjoy having time to play with others, a playdate now is really a chance for you to take a break.

When arranging playdates, it's best to stick with one-on-one events. For the most part, don't expect your child to play with the other child. Parallel play, or playing next to each other, is more likely. If you watch your child with another child, you will see them stealing looks at each other, imitating each other's actions, and of course showing interest in each other's things.

When you do take your child for a playdate or invite a playmate to your house, use the following tips to enhance the encounter:

♦ Keep the playdate short. About an hour is as long as most toddlers can handle.

♦ Plan activities that don't involve sharing. If possible, provide two of each kind of toy to cut down on territorial tussles.

♦ Stay close. Your toddler's favorite playmates this year are the grown-ups she trusts, and she'll want you or her caregiver close by when another playmate enters the picture. It's not necessary to hover, however, since your child needs to see that you have confidence that she will learn to be sociable on her own. Be available to suggest play and to interfere with any acts of aggression.

♦ Respect your child's social style. You may find that your child rushes into each new situation, hangs back and observes before joining in, or plays best from the comfort of your lap. While gently encouraging interaction, respect your child's personal comfort level.

Respect your child's uniqueness

All children learn to walk and talk, think—and feel— at their own unique pace. Always remember to respect your child's timetable, support her development, be patient—and savor this exciting journey.